Volcanoes in Iceland

Ari Trausti Guðmundsson

Volcanoes in Iceland

10.000 Years of Volcanic History

Vaka-Helgafell

VOLCANOES IN ICELAND

Published by Vaka-Helgafell,
Reykjavík 1996
Printed in Portugal

Information address:
Vaka-Helgafell hf.,
Sidumuli 6, 108 Reykjavik, Iceland
E-mail vaka@itn is

ISBN 9979-2-0348-X

Table of Contents

Foreword

There are not only many volcanoes in Iceland, but they differ in size, appearance and nature. The volcanoes have a very long history, which is often complicated and not easily traced. Much has been written on recent volcanic activity in Iceland. Some of the literature dates back to the 18th and 19th centuries, and old annals and other written sources as far back as the 13th century. Most of the relevant information, however, is contained in hundreds of scientific magazine articles published during the past few decades, in Icelandic or English. They usually deal with specific volcanic areas, certain volcanoes, eruptions or volcanic phenomena, but very few cover volcanism in Iceland in general. An outline of the volcanic history written by Þorvaldur Thoroddsen, "Die Gesichte der isländischen Vulkane", was published in 1925 (in German), and "Íslandseldar", a review of all the volcanic systems in Iceland by this writer, was published in 1986 (in Icelandic).

Useful references to magazine articles, scientific papers and chapters in books, dealing with Icelandic volcanism, are found in a list of selected references. These writings can be utilized as a guide to further references.

This book is partly based on "Íslandseldar" and partly on new information obtained by scientists since 1986. I have tried to outline the most important aspects of the volcanic history within the limited space of the following pages, aided by photographs, maps and other graphic illustrations. The sources of the graphic illustrations are listed and acknowledged on pages 130 and 131. This book is meant to be of interest to people without knowledge of geology, but also relevant to scientists or students who need an outline of the volcanic activity in Iceland.

I wish to thank geologists Dr. Ágúst Guðmundsson and Dr. Haukur Jóhannesson for their review and helpful comments, Mr. Don Brandt and Mr. Rab Christie for correcting the English, the numerous photographers for their contribution and the publisher Vaka-Helgafell for fruitful cooperation.

Ari Trausti Guðmundsson

Introduction

For scientists and laymen alike, Iceland offers unique opportunities to study various types of volcanic activity and related structures or processes. The interaction of man and volcanoes is demontrated not only by history but also by the frequent eruptions that disturb or delight people living in or visiting Iceland. This introduction serves as a shortcut to chapters 1-19, describing the main volcanic areas and volcanoes of Iceland. In the last chapter of the book (Chapter 20) there is a more thorough overview of the roots of Icelandic volcanism, some petrological aspects and a classification of eruptives and volcanic structures.

A visible part of an oceanic rift-system

We think that volcanism in Iceland has been more or less uniform for the past 15 million years or so. Man has been around in Iceland for only 1,100-1,200 years; a mere trifle seen in that context. In that time, however, we have learnt to understand the volcanic activity in the country and experienced how to live amongst active volcanoes. The volcanic activity is confined to a zone that dissects Iceland, totalling with flank zones some 1/4 of the island area. We see the

1. Volcanic activity is not only an interesting subject for research, but also a wonderful feature to watch. Fluid lava, Krafla Fires 1975–1984. (Photo: Sigurður Þórarinsson)

active volcanic zone as the furrow (rift zone) of the Mid-Atlantic Ridge across Iceland. In the North Atlantic, this huge submarine structure is the edge of two immense plates that drift in opposite directions. A part of it is elevated above sea level in Iceland due to the presence of a magma-rich mantle plume (hot spot). There, we can study the rift-type, oceanic volcanism and related tectonic or geothermal processes. And more than that; the hot spot and the volcanic flank zones allow us to glimpse other types of volcanic activity and structures more related to continental volcanism than are usually found at oceanic rift zones.

■ One eruption every fourth year

In historical time, since AD850-900, more than 250 volcanic eruptions have occurred in Iceland. The individual volcanoes and volcanic fissures number a few hundred but they group into 30 distinct volcanic systems. Each system comprises open tectonic fissures, faults, volcanic structures like crater rows or lava shields and most of the systems include a volcanic centre. Some of these are volcanic massifs with a caldera structure, others are cone-shaped stratovolcanoes. All these formations along with vast lava flows give the landscape of the active volcanic zone a distinct flavour or look. A lunar landscape, some say, but others are fascinated by the encounter between the earthly fires and ice of the heavily glaciated highlands.

Even the formerly active volcanic areas, now located east and west of the rift zone (due to the plate movements), are characterized by ice and fire because the thick lava stacks are eroded by Ice Age glaciers. There, we can study the internal structure of volcanoes and lava sequences; walk into the wombs of the "infernal machines" as some medieval scholars used to label the volcanoes.

■ A noteable neighbour

The early settlers of Iceland were soon greeted by volcanic unrest. Powerful and disturbing eruptions like in Vatnaöldur around AD871, Eldgjá in AD934 and Hekla in 1104 must have created mixed emotions among people and caused damage. All the same, most of these events did not enter the manuscripts and sagas made from the early 12th century until other types of written sources took over. And the defying blasts and widespread lava flows occurring in the 14th to 17th century only earned a few clipped sentences in the books. In the 18th and 19th centuries more lengthy and accurate accounts were made of a number of eruptions. They clearly illustrate that the volcanoes were not only neighbours to respect but did influence the course of history and the economic development to a considerable extent. The „Haze Famine" (Laki-eruption) in the late 18th century dealt a heavy blow to the Icelandic community. Only a few decades ago, the Heimaey-eruption almost wiped out a large town and made headlines the world over, as Icelandic volcanoes have done a few times before our days.

■ Knowledge helps

The inevitable task of learning to live with volcanoes awaits Icelanders every year as time passes. What was once met with religious faith only or the stoic calmness of people living in close contact with nature is now being encountered also with science. Geological

2. The blazing crater of Eldfell. The Heimaey eruption in 1973 soon became centralized to this scoria and tephra cone which attained a height of 220 m. (Photo: Skúli Víkingsson)

research, geophysical data and various high-tech instruments help to create a fairly good picture of Icelandic volcanism. One of the aims of this scientific work is to faciliate predictions of volcanic eruptions. The task of monitoring volcanoes and to slowly improve predictions of eruptions is a never-ending one. Some of the knowledge already acquired is presented in this book.

Each of the following chapters deals with one or a few volcanic systems. The last chapter, however, is centered around processes in mantle, the mechanisms of volcano-tectonic events, petrological aspects and the classification of volcanoes, eruptives etc. Some readers may wish to start reading that chapter, which gives some scientific base for further reading but others may leave this chapter out or use it as concluding reading material.

■ Watching volcanoes

The following institutions participate in volcanological research:
The Geoscience Dept. of the University of Iceland.
The University of Iceland
Hringbraut, 101 Reykjavík,
tel. 525 4000 – fax 525 4499

The Museum of Natural History
Hlemmur 3, 101 Reykjavík,
tel. 562 9822 – fax 562 0815

The Science Institute of the University of Iceland
Dunhagi 3, 107 Reykjavík,
tel. 525 4800 – fax 552 8911

The National Energy Authority
Grensásvegur 9, 108 Reykjavík,
tel. 569 6000 – fax 568 8896

The Nordic Volcanological Institute
The Geoscience Building
University of Iceland
Hringbraut, 101 Reykjavík,
tel. 525 4491 – fax 562 9767

The Geophysical Department of the Meteorological Office of Iceland
Bústaðavegi 9
108 Reykjavík
tel. 560 0600 – fax. 552 5411

Instructive Eruptions

The Icelanders learnt a lot about the behaviour of fissure swarms and central volcanoes during the Krafla Fires at 1975-1984. Crustal dilation to an order of many metres, subterranean magma flows and nine surface fissure eruptions partly revealed how the plate tectonics work in Iceland. The nearby Lake Mývatn was created during a similar episode more than 2,000 years ago.

■ A restless volcano

Lake Mývatn is one of Nature's paradises. The lush vegetation, a lake full of life, abundant birds and interesting geological formations have made the lake and its surroundings famous as a tourist resort. The lake owes its existence and much of its uniqueness to the volcanic system which runs parallel to its eastern shores. Fissures, faults and crater rows characterize the landscape, along with two large tephra rings and geothermal fields.

The Mývatn fissure swarm is the southern section of the Krafla Volcanic System (Fig. 8 and 13). Rootless vents or pseudocraters dot the lake shores and form small islands (Fig. 7). Rootless crater cones form when fluid lava flows over wetlands, lakes and water-soaked

3. The Víti maar in the Krafla caldera. The Mývatn Fires (1724-1729) started with a very short phreatic eruption, creating the "Hellhole". (Photo: Halldór Kjartansson)

sediments. Bizarre lava formations such as the Dimmuborgir lava labyrinth and Kálfastrandarstrípar add further dimensions to the Mývatn area.

The centre of the volcanic system is a cluster of low ridges and individual mountains formed during the Pleistocene (younger than 200,000 years), northeast of Lake Mývatn. The volcanic centre has developed a caldera which is partly filled with young volcanic rocks. A powerful high-temperature geothermal field is located in the caldera. Small hyaloclastite mountains, Krafla and Leirhnjúkur, are also within the caldera. The central volcano (the Krafla volcano) has derived its name from the Krafla mountain (Fig. 13 and 97).

The northern section of the fissure swarm is very distinct due to Gjástykki, a large downfaulted valley (graben) with walls up to 30 m high. Crater rows stretch up to 35 km to the north from the centre and the faults even farther into the sea at the Öxarfjörður bay.

■ The creation of lake Mývatn

The total length of the active fissure swarm of the Krafla Volcanic System is 90 km. It is 3-8 km wide. The caldera

4. Some 2,800 years ago, a short but powerful tephra eruption initiated the ongoing Hverfjall (or Hverfell) Period in the Krafla Volcanic System. The crater, a tephra ring, measures 1,000 m in diameter. (Photo: Ragnar Th. Sigurðsson)

5. The volcano-tectonic event of the Krafla Fires, January 1981. This was the seventh of eventually nine eruptions during this 9 year-long episode. Lava fountains and fast-flowing "lava rivers" characterized the events. (Photo: Ómar Þ. Ragnarsson)

itself measures 10 by 8 km. Many crater rows are in the swarm, as well as tephra rings and explosive craters (maars), for example Víti (Fig. 3) to the north of the Krafla Geothermal Power Station (30 MW, steam turbine-powered). Víti dates from 1724 when a rifting episode started with an explosive eruption. The episode gave rise to at least 7 fissure eruptions, mainly in the caldera, and many earthquakes (a series of volcano-tectonic events), and lasted until 1729. The fissure swarm widened considerably. The discontinuous active fissure section became 10 km long and each subsequent eruption produced a lava flow. The lava reached the farming district on the northeastern shore of Mývatn. The total area of the lava is 33 km^2 and the volume about 0.25 km^3.

Prior to this episode, a series of eruptions occurred in the southern section of the fissure swarm (0.2 km^3 of lava), the so-called Dalseldar Fires, around AD900. About 2,300-2,500 years ago (2,500 BP = Before present) a long-lasting rifting episode (Hólseldar) led to the formation of the 8 km-long crater row of Lúdentsborgir and Þrengslaborgir and a few more volcanic fissures as well. It must be noted that the Lúdent-Þrengslaborgir area probably constitutes, along with other fissures, faults and craters in the neighbourhood, an individual fissure swarm or volcanic system (Heiðarsporður Volcanic System). The lava from Lúdentsborgir and Þrengslaborgir flowed over the old Mývatn lake in the shallow depression east of the fissures, creating the present lake. The lava (Laxárhraun yngra) has a volume of 3-4 km^3 (an area over 200 km^2) and flowed all the way to the Skjálfandi Bay, 70 km away.

Some 300 years before the Hólseldar episode a short, forceful tephra eruption created the Hverfjall (or Hverfell) tephra ring (2,600-2,800 years ago, 1,000 m diameter, Fig. 4). It was followed by fissure lava eruptions which created among other features the Kerlingarhólar lava field, 25 km north of the caldera. Together all these episodes, and the late Krafla Fires, constitute a 2,800 year-long volcano-tectonic period: the Hverfjall Period.

■ The many Krafla Fires

The present volcanic period in the Krafla volcanic system began with the Hverfjall eruption. The period includes at least 5 rifting episodes and associated eruptions, mentioned above. Prior to the Hverfjall Period, from about 7,500 to at least 11,000 years ago, a similar volcanic period (the Lúdent Period) prevailed in the Krafla volcanic system (and partly in the Heiðarsporður system if counted as an individual one). The period includes a Hverfjall-like eruption, creating the tephra ring Lúdent, east of Hverfjall. Other volcanic episodes in that period include eruptions at Námafjall, Kröfluháls and near Lúdent. In between the Hverfjall and Lúdent Periods some rifting took place in the Krafla system, but seemingly only one small eruption occurred.

The latest addition to the volcano-tectonic episodes in the Hverfjall Period dates from 1975 to 1984. In September 1975 many earthquakes shook the earth in the Krafla region and in the northern section of the fissure swarm. The seismic activity became more intense in late December, and by the end of December 250 earthquakes larger than 3.5 (Richter scale) and 10 larger than 4.0 had occurred in the swarm. A tiny volcanic eruption followed (on Dec. 20), north of the Krafla Power Station.

The total widening of the fissure swarm amounts to 8-9 m, corresponding to a sudden movement due to the release of stresses at the local plate boundaries, after 250 years of little or no movement (since the Mývatn Fires in the 18th century).

During the following nine years, magma flowed into a magma chamber at Krafla, which is at a depth of 3-7 km depth, at a minimum rate of 5 m^3 per second. The chamber, which is probably the eastern one of two such chambers, inflated due to the in-flow, and then deflated as magma was injected into the fissure swarm at least 21 times over. The land elevation changes were measurable. Sometimes, the magma flowed south along fissures (forming dykes) but never surfaced, except once through a borehole! More often, it flowed northwards through fissures (forming dykes), and during nine of the events some magma surfaced on discontinuous fissures in fire-fountain eruptions of highly fluid basaltic lava (once in 1975, twice in 1977, three times in 1980, twice in 1981, and once in 1984, which was the largest eruption, Fig. 5 and 6). Scientists were able to forecast most of the eruptions. Although the geothermal activity was affected and boreholes were damaged, the power station resumed production after a temporary halt.

The ninth eruption in 1984 started on April 4th 1984. At 20.40 in the evening,

6. Basaltic lava fountains from off-set (en echelon) fissure segments during the volcano-tectonic event in January 1981 at Krafla. (Photo: Ómar Þ. Ragnarsson)

7. Rootless craters (pseudocraters) at Lake Mývatn. They were formed more than 2,000 years ago as lava entered the old Lake Mývatn and steam blasts and degassing created the cones.

(Photo: Rafn Hafnfjörð)

tiltmeters registered a deflation of the magma chamber, and 15 minutes later earth tremors showed on local seismometers. The first low-frequency earthquake was registered at 23.40, indicating that magma was forcing its way through the upper crust. Nine minutes later, people noticed a reddish glow in the sky north of Krafla. Within another 20 minutes, the earth's surface split up along two 2 km-long fissure segments and red-hot lava fountains rose up to 150 m into the air. More fissure segments opened up during the next hour or so north and south of the initial vents, and finally eight segments formed a blazing eruptive fissure which stretched from Leirhnúkur, some 8.5 km to the North. The subsidence of the earth's surface stopped the next day, but commenced a few days later until the eruption ceased on September 18th (totalling 5 cm). Soon, some of the spatter cones became extinct and a few other craters started to spout steam and tephra instead of fluid basalt lava, which continued to flow from the main craters. The lava flow has an area of 24 km^2

■ The episode may not be over

The volcanic fissures of each of the nine eruptions (events) of the Krafla Fires have opened up inside the caldera and, in most cases, propagated in a sideways-shifted fashion (en echelon) northwards in the course of each eruption, up to 8.5 km from the caldera rim. The first four eruptions produced only 0.4-3.0 million m^3 of lava each, on short fissures. The subsequent five more forceful eruptions formed longer crater rows which emitted 20-90 million m^3 (0.09 km^3) of lava each, covering as much as 24 km^2. The total lava cover from all nine eruptions is 66 km^2 (0.25-0.30 km^3).

A marked chemical difference between lavas simultaneously erupted inside and outside the caldera suggests that evolved magma from the crustal magma chamber reaches not far from its source, and that the less evolved distant lava flows may stem from the deeper reservoir underlying most of the length of the volcanic system.

Currently, Krafla's magma chamber is inflated to a high level. Everything has, however, remained more or less calm in the area for some 10 years. This does not necessarily imply that the Krafla Fires are definitely over, but measurements of slow deflation indicate a contraction of the magma chamber.

8. The Krafla Volcanic System from the air. Fissures, normal faults (a graben) and hyaloclastite ridges mark the northern part of the fissure swarm. The table mountain (stapi) to the right is Gæsafjöll. The caldera lies east (left) of the mountain.

(Photo: Oddur Sigurðsson)

Iceland's most active Volcano

Grímsvötn has been regarded as Iceland's most active central volcano, erupting every 10-15 years on average. Its caldera is located in the Vatnajökull ice cap and contains a subglacial lake. Geothermal activity melts the overlying ice. The rising lake level or occasional volcanic eruptions cause jökulhlaups (glacier bursts; floods) which sweep the black sand deserts in front of the Skeiðarárjökull outlet glacier.

■ "The burning lakes"

According to folk tales, Grímsvötn in the Vatnajökull ice cap (8,300 km^2) is the home of trolls and giants where "lakes burn". In fact, Grímsvötn is a hidden caldera lake beneath a 200-250 m-thick floating ice sheet in a central volcano. The glacial ice completely overruns the northern caldera walls but 200-400 m rock and ice walls rim the caldera to the south at Grímsfjall where two gentle peaks (Svíahnúkar) reach the altitudes of 1,700 and 1,725 m (Fig. 12).

A very powerful high-temperature geothermal area is active beneath the snow and ice, issuing steam through vents in the snowfields. The geothermal

9. The small tephra eruption in Grímsvötn in 1983 below the southern caldera rim. A small island was seen in the breach in the ice shelf. (Photo: Oddur Sigurðsson)

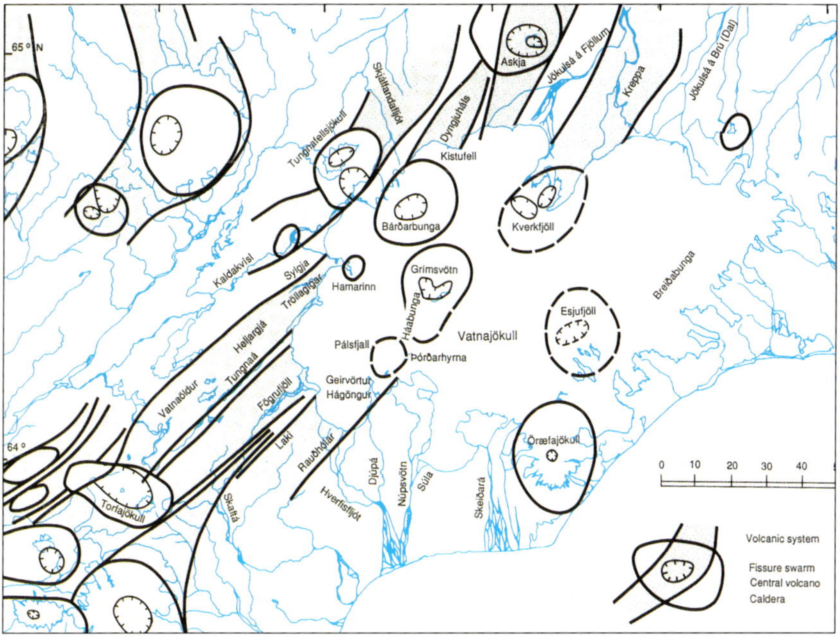

10. The volcanic centres within the Vatnajökull ice cap. Parts of fissure swarms, outside the ice cap, are also shown (grey, with black borders). The Loki centre is proposed between Grímsvötn and Bárðarbunga/Hamarinn.

area is heated by a shallow magma chamber beneath the caldera and by dykes which have been injected into the crust above the chamber. Tephra eruptions occur every 10-20 years on average, probably making Grímsvötn the most active volcano in Iceland.

The caldera complex of the Grímsvötn central volcano (Fig. 13) includes a 600 m-deep main caldera (20 km^2) and another intersecting one, to the north and west of the main structure (about 15 km^2). The bottom of the main caldera is composed of tephra layers and a thick series of lava-like structures and mounds.

■ The caldera overflows

The subglacial caldera lake owes its existence to a strong heat flux from the magma beneath Grímsvötn. Ice flowing into the caldera melts in large quantities. This source of water, and other sources such as surface snow melting (ablation) and steam or water from the geothermal vents, supply the lake with 20 m^3 of water per second. The lake has an area of 8-10 km^2 or more (Fig. 13). The lake level rises slowly until the lake is partly emptied during successive glacier bursts. The water depth may vary from 40 to 200 m. The ice sheet on the lake has been 150-250 m thick during the past decades, depending on glacier balance and ice flow.

Prior to a glacier burst from Grímsvötn, the rising level of the lake lifts the ice sheet until a critical point is reached. Then the pressure at the lake bottom causes a subglacial waterway to

11. North-south cross-section of the Grímsvötn main caldera. The open water at the foot of Grímsfjall (Vestari-Svíahnúkur) is at the site of the 1983 eruption.

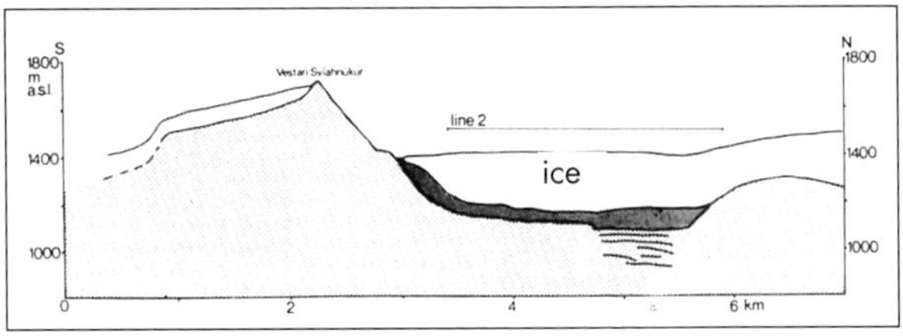

open at the glacier's bed. Heat from the friction of the rushing water keeps the waterway open. The water flows more than 50 km beneath the Skeiðarárjökull outlet glacier until it reaches the river Skeiðará in Skaftafell National Park. The lake drains until the ice pressure closes the waterway as the ice shelf slowly sinks and cracks, usually 1-3 weeks later (Fig. 14).

From 1629 (first reliable reference) until after a volcanic eruption of 1934, these glacier bursts occurred once every 10 years, with a volume of up to 5 km^3 and a discharge of up to tens of thousands of cubic metres per second. Since 1934 bursts have been recorded every 4-6 years. They are generally declining, now with less than half the former volume and discharge of 2,000-3,000 m^3/s. Each volcanic eruption, however, enhances the ice melting and stimulates the geothermal activity for a relatively brief period. Furthermore, eruptions may cause single bursts to be extra large or even disturb the overflow time pattern (Table p. 21).

■ Iceland's most active volcano

The past two decades have been rather chilly in Iceland. During that time, the floating ice sheet in Grímsvötn has become thicker and thus heavier to lift, and a few very small eruptions since 1934-1938 have not supplied the geothermal field with as much heat as the larger eruptions prior to that. From 1860 to 1934, volcanic eruptions every tenth year increased the power of the geothermal area to 4,000-5,500 MW instead of the present 2,500-3,000 MW.

Written sources on historical eruptions and glacier bursts in Grímsvötn date back to 1332. Tephra layers suggest that at least a few volcanic eruptions occurred earlier. Tephra layers also suggest more eruptions in Grímsvötn during the past 3-4 centuries than those found in written sources, no doubt due to the volcano's remoteness. All in all, at least 40-50 eruptions have occurred in Grímsvötn in historical time, of which 36 (in or near Grímsvötn) are certain or very likely. Most were small, with a tephra production of 50-100 million m^3 (0.05-0.1 km^3), but in between were larger and more violent eruptions. Two recorded eruptions occurred in 1934 and 1938 (a large eruption north of the main caldera) and the two latest ones in 1983 (Fig. 9 and 11) and 1984, but of much smaller magnitude.

The volume of eruptives since 1600 is estimated as 2.3 km^3 but may be in order of 3-5 km^3 in historical time. The recent Holocene volcanic history prior to the settlement of Iceland, indicated by tephra layers, is more or less unknown.

■ Other volcanoes in Vatnajökull

There are no visible indications of a fissure swarm which can without any doubt

12. The site of the 1934 eruption (view to Grímsfjall). Note the lake with ice floes and black tephra. (Photo: R. Leutelt)

be traced to Grímsvötn. Most of the area is covered with ice. But long volcanic fissures in front of the Síðujökull glacier (at Vatnajökull's southwestern margin), such as the Laki fissure, are aligned to Grímsvötn and might certainly form a volcanic system along with the ice-clad centre. This might also be deduced from the somewhat similar chemical content of eruptives from Grímsvötn and the Laki fissure, as well as accounts of simultaneous eruptions on that fissure and in the Grímsvötn area. Scientists debate whether the magma of the Laki fissure was extruded from Grímsvötn's magma chamber or not, and furthermore, if not, how it relates to a reservoir below the volcanic fissure. An associated caldera formation in Grímsvötn has been suggested.

Other written accounts suggest volcanic activity north and west of Grímsvötn. Today two large ice cauldrons appear west of Grímsvötn. Beneath them is the geothermal source of small glacier bursts appearing in the Skaftá river and also the site of small, totally subglacial eruptions. The term Loki Volcanic System has been proposed. (Fig. 10)

South of Grímsvötn a glaciated cluster of peaks is regarded as a central volcano, called the Þórðarhyrna volcano. It seems to be the centre of a small volcanic system with crater rows south and southwest of the Síðujökull glacier. These are all older than 2,000-4,000 years, but there are accounts of glacier bursts and subglacial eruptions in the 18th, 19th and probably early 20th centuries which point towards volcanic activity near Þórðarhyrna. North of Grímsvötn is the Kverkfjöll central volcano (see Chapter 15).

The Grímsvötn central volcano is monitored and measurements are made each year to establish the rising level of the subglacial lake and to reveal the structure of the volcano.

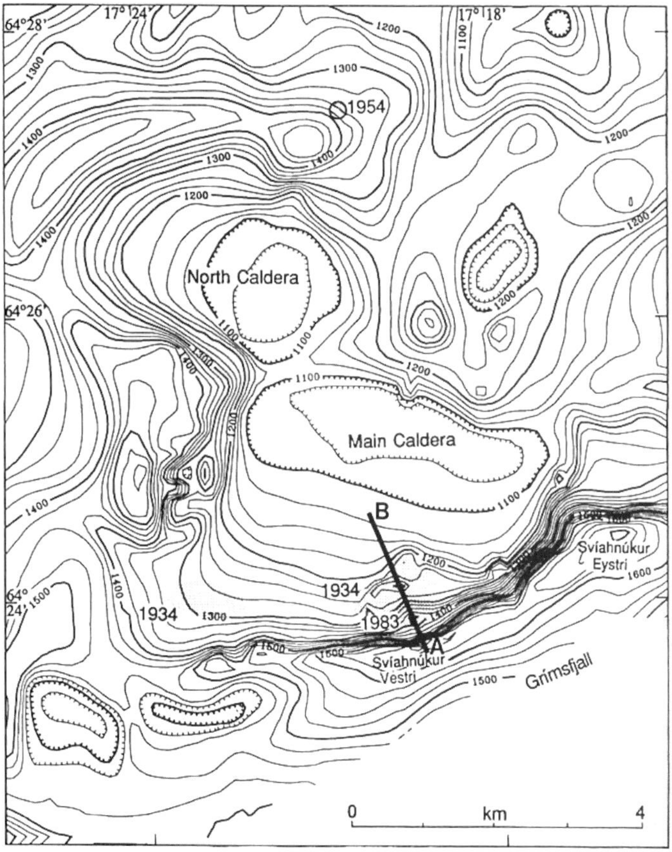

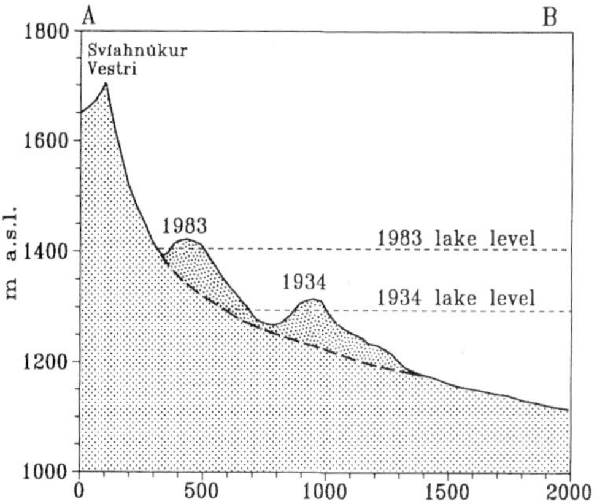

13. Grímsvötn, the central volcano in the Vatnajökull ice cap: bedrock as revealed by radioecho soundings and seismic reflection surveys. Contour interval is 25 m. Shaded areas denote the eruption sites in 1934 and 1983. The eruption site in 1938 is well north of the North Caldera and the 1954 sign denotes a large sinkhole, appearing in that year. A-B is a cross-section, shown at left.

RECORDED, HISTORICAL VOLCANIC ERUPTIONS AND GLACIER BURSTS IN THE GRÍMSVÖTN VOLCANIC SYSTEM

Year	Location	Glacier burst
*905	Grímsvötn system	unknown
*1060	Grímsvötn system	unknown
1332	(Grímsvötn)	(Skeiðará)
1341	(Grímsvötn)	unknown
*1354	Grímsvötn system	unknown
*1500	Grímsvötn system	unknown
1598	Grímsvötn	unknown
1603	(Grímsvötn system)	unknown
1619	Grímsvötn	unknown
1629	Grímsvötn	Skeiðará
1638	Grímsvötn	Skeiðará
1659	Grímsvötn	(Skeiðará)
1684-85	Grímsvötn	Skeiðará
1706	(Grímsvötn)	(Skeiðará)
1716	(Grímsvötn system)	Jökulsá á Fjöllum
1725	Grímsvötn	Skeiðará
1753	Grímsvötn system	Skaftá, Hverfisfljót
1769	(Grímsvötn)	Þjórsá
1774	Grímsvötn	Skeiðará
1783	Grímsvötn system	Skaftá, Tungnaá
1784-85	Grímsvötn system	Núpsvötn, Skeiðará
1816	(Grímsvötn)	unknown
1823	Grímsvötn (+)	unknown
1838	Grímsvötn	Skeiðará
1854	Grímsvötn system	unknown
1861 ?	(Grímsvötn)	Skeiðará
1867	Grímsvötn (+)	Skeiðará
1873	Grímsvötn (+)	Skeiðará, Djúpá
1883	Grímsvötn (+)	Skeiðará
1892	Grímsvötn	Skeiðará
1897	(Grímsvötn)	Skeiðará
1903	(Grímsvötn) (+)	Skeiðará, Súla
1922	Grímsvötn	Skeiðará, Súla
1933	N of Grímsvötn	none
1934	Grímsvötn	Skeiðará, Súla
1938	N of Grímsvötn	Skeiðará, Súla
1939 ?	Grímsvötn	Skeiðará
1941 ?	Grímsvötn	Skeiðará
1945 ?	Grímsvötn	Skeiðará
1954 ?	N of Grímsvötn	Skeiðará
1983	Grímsvötn	none
1984 ?	Grímsvötn	none

* denotes an uncertain year, ? an uncertain event, () an uncertain location, (+) additional activity in nearby volcanoes.

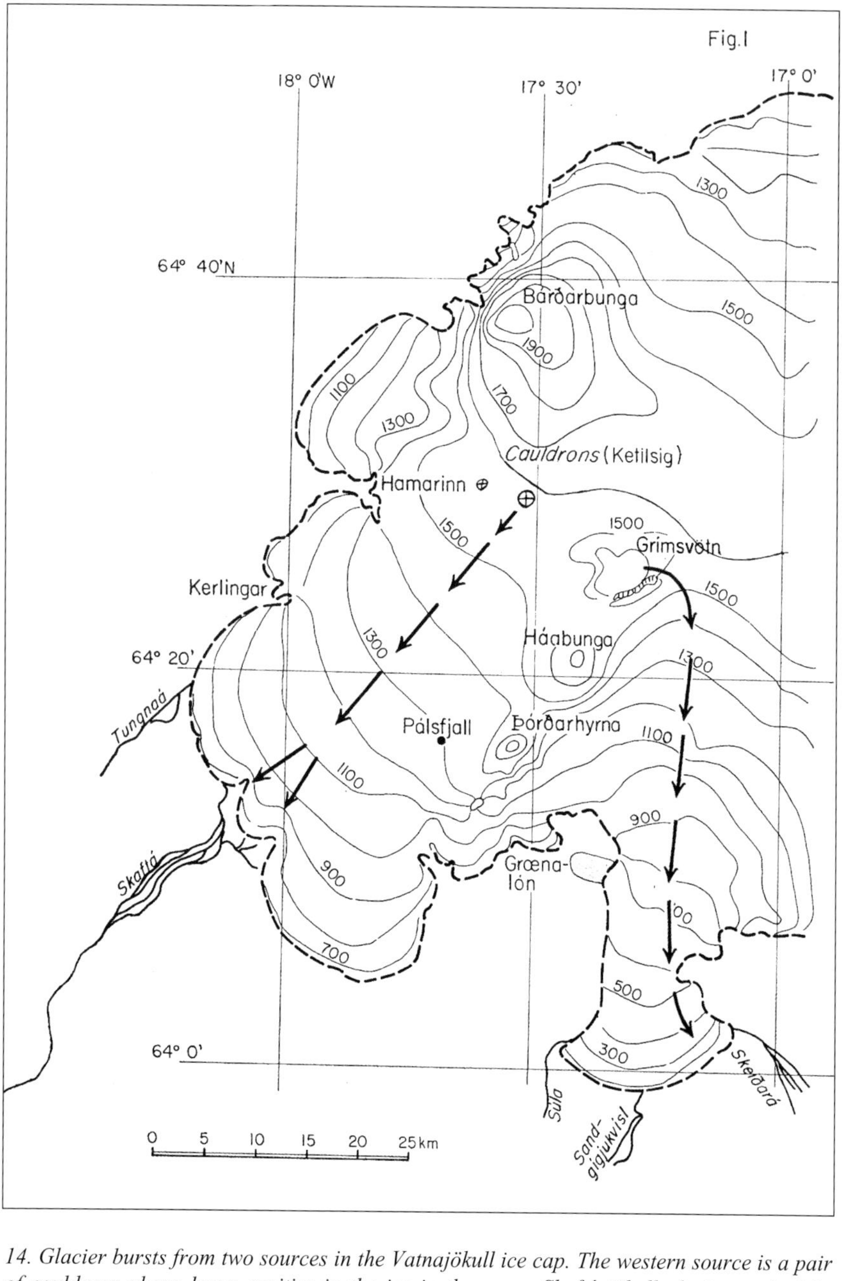

14. Glacier bursts from two sources in the Vatnajökull ice cap. The western source is a pair of cauldrons above large cavities in the ice in the upper Skaftárjökull glacier, melted by geothermal heat in the Loki Volcanic System. The eastern source is the lake in the Grímsvötn main caldera. There, ice is melted by geothermal heat or volcanic eruptions. The floodwater flows beneath the Skeiðarárjökull glacier.

The Group of Fire Islands

All 18 of the islands, sea stacks and skerries forming the Vestmannaeyjar group are of young, volcanic origin. Heimaey, the largest island, is home to 5,000 people. Two recent eruptions in Vestmannaeyjar made headlines the world over: the submarine eruption and the birth of Surtsey island in 1963-1967, and the fissure eruption on Heimaey. Currently, the volcanic system of Vestmannaeyjar is under constant surveillance.

■ Beautiful islands

The 18 islands, stacks and skerries that rise from the restless North Atlantic Ocean, 10-20 km off the south coast of Iceland, are truly a fine sight. The largest and only inhabited island is called Heimaey, 11 km^2. It is the home of 5,000 people and Iceland's largest fishing town (Fig. 19).

The main rock in Vestmannaeyjar is basaltic hyaloclastite, indicating that the islands originated in subglacial or submarine eruptions. The Pleistocene glaciers reached the Vestmannaeyjar area, but most of the larger islands are of postglacial age. They were formed in postglacial (Holocene) submarine eruptions which primarily produced tephra (phreatic eruptions), for example, Álsey and Hellisey islands, 8,000 years ago, and Elliðaey, Bjarnarey and parts of Heimaey, 5,000-6,000 years ago or less.

In historical times, only two uncertain submarine eruptions occurred near

15. Only some 400 m separated the easternmost houses in the town on Heimaey from the lava fountains of the new volcanic fissure (the first day of the eruption).
(Photo: Ari Trausti Guðmundsson)

16. Two phases of the Surtsey eruption 1963-1967. Left: The initial tephra-producing phase. Phreatic eruption with steam and tephra clouds. Right: As soon as the sea did not enter the volcanic vent, an effusive lava-producing phase started. (Photos: Sigurður Þórarinsson)

Vestmannaeyjar in 1637 and in 1896, but neither led to the formation of an island.

■About 80 volcanic sites

Evolved, intermediate eruptives of Heimaey (from the alkalic series) indicate that the main island is slowly developing into a volcanic centre. Approximately 80 volcanic sites, above and below sea level, group around it and form a 38 km-long and 30 km-wide volcanic system (Fig. 17). Measurements suggest a deep magma source 10-30 km beneath the surface where conditions facilitate the generation of the alkali basalts and related magma.

Submarine volcanic sites are found east of Vestmannaeyjar (Háfadjúp). The Vestmannaeyjar Volcanic System forms the south end of the Eastern Volcanic Zone.

After a seemingly lengthy period of inactivity, up to 5,000 years or probably less, disregarding two uncertain eruptions, the very recent eruptions in Vestmannaeyjar came as a surprise. In

1967, the Surtsey eruption made headlines the world over, as did the Heimaey eruption in 1973.

■ A large island born in 42 months

In late 1963 an eruption started about 20 km southwest of Heimaey (Fig. 16). A 500 m-long fissure opened up on the sea floor, 130 m below sea level. Black tephra columns rose from the sea for five months and built up a sizeable island, 170 m high. Three satellite islands (Jólnir, Syrtlingur and the more or less submerged Surtla) formed on fissures parallel to the main one, but the battering waves swept them away as soon as the short-lived and phreatic eruptions ceased. When the sea could no longer flow into the main volcanic vent on the main island, the eruption changed from an explosive tephra eruption to an effusive eruption of very fluid, basaltic lava. It formed a cap of ropy lava (pahoehoe) on the island which was named Surtsey after the giant Surtur in ancient Nordic mythology.

The lava eruption continued with short breaks until mid-year 1967. All this resistant lava and the hardening tuffs ensured a long life for Surtsey. The island had an area of 2.7 km^2, but the volume of the pyramid-like volcano was 1.1 km^3.

Today, Surtsey is already heavily eroded by waves and wind and its area is about 1.5 km^2 or 56% of the original size. The virgin island is the site of biological and geological research. The biologists follow the development of new life taking to the volcanic structure, both above and below sea level. Geologists study, for example, morphological processes and lava caves or pioneer important research on how the tuff is transformed to hard rock (palagonitization).

■ The narrow escape

Ten years later, a volcanic fissure tore up the bedrock of Vestmannaeyjar. The rift sliced up the eastern part of Heimaey, only 300-400 m away from

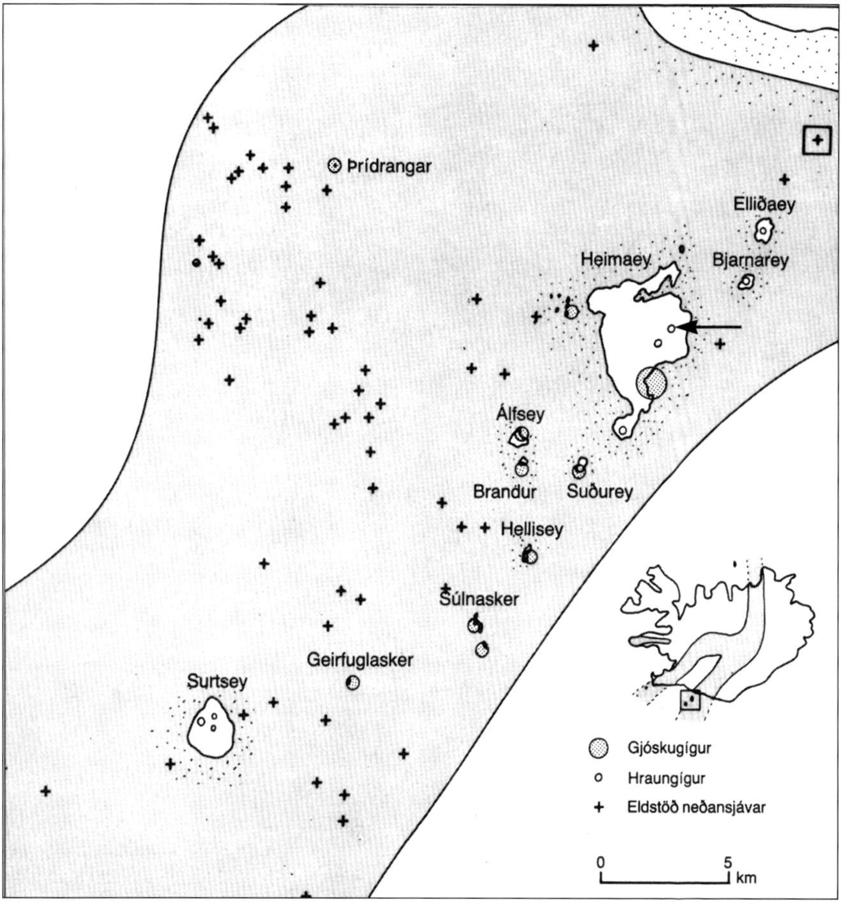

17. The active Vestmannaeyjar Volcanic System. Some 80 postglacial (Holocene) submarine (crosses) volcanic sites and islands are shown here. Large circles denote tephra craters and small dots are lava craters. The square shows a submarine volcanic vent from 1973. The main crater from 1973 (Eldfell) is indicated by an arrow.

the edge of the town (Fig. 18). Luckily, most of the fishing fleet was in harbour and the wind was westerly. In a few hours, the inhabitants of Vestmannaeyjar escaped to the mainland and no lives were lost or serious injuries inflicted. One person perished later during the eruption.

The lava fountains soon became localized at the central section of the fissure, and there a 220 m-high scoria cone formed in a few months (Eldfell). Lava bombs and large tephra lumps damaged houses or set fire to them, and later on, the very thick, slow-moving lava (hawaiite) crept over many houses

18. The early hours on the first day of the Heimaey eruption in 1973. The few-thousand-year-old Helgafell scoria cone is seen to the left of the main eruption on the new fissure. (Photo: Ingibjörg Kaldal)

19. The town of Vestmannaeyjar on the Heimaey island. The Eldfell volcano to the right and Bjarnarey and Elliðaey volcanic islands along with Mt. Eyjafjallajökull in the background.
(Photo: Mats Vibe Lund)

(Fig. 2 and 15). Attempts to cool the lava front by spraying it with sea-water were successful in slowing down the flow.

The volcanic activity continued for five months as a mixed eruption of lava and tephra. Nearly 200 houses were buried by the lava or very thick pumice. With domestic and international aid and extensive clean-up work, the town regained its former position and wealth.

The eruptive volume of the Heimaey eruption was 0.25-0.30 km^3 and the lava covers 2.3 km^2.

■ The future

Currently, monitoring instruments keep track of seismic activity and crustal deformation in the Vestmannaeyjar islands. So far, there have not been any signs of imminent danger. The volcanic system is, however, very young, and as yet has no central volcano. Fissure eruptions on the sea floor and on Heimaey will, undoubtedly, continue to occur in the future. A new strip of land, possibly connected to the mainland, may thus start to form where Heimaey is now. Heimaey will turn into a central volcano. The time-scale for this development is, however, tens and hundreds of thousands of years.

The Diverging Margins

To actually see and study the system of fissures and faults of a graben on the crest of the Mid-Atlantic Rift System that is a truly a spectacular sight. At Þingvellir, the site of the ancient parliament of Iceland, a tectonic showcase draws thousands upon thousands of people to enjoy Nature. Close by, the volcanic centre of Hengill boosts the newest addition to the geothermal installations in Iceland; the Nesjavellir power plant.

■ Where West meets East

One of the best locations for observing the rift zones that characterize the divergent plate margins of the Earth is at Þingvellir. It is a flat area covered by large lava flows, overgrown with mosses, willows, heather and birches, above the northeastern shores of Lake Þingvallavatn. Huge faults and large fissures showing continuous movement cut through the lava (Fig. 20). Together they form a 7 km-wide valley, less than 10,000 years old, with a slowly sinking floor (graben). Recent fault walls about 30 m high (e.g. at Almannagjá) and fissures up to 5-10 m wide bear witness to the immense forces which pull the plates apart in the rift zones. But the area is not only famous as a tectonic showcase.

20. Almannagjá in Þingvellir National Park is a big normal fault located within the active fissure swarm of the Hengill Volcanic System. It is formed by tensional stresses and related crustal rifting as the western boundary of a 5-7 km-wide graben. (Photo: Halldór Kjartansson)

This ancient site of the old Icelandic parliament (founded in AD930) is well known for nearby volcanoes. Fissures have poured out large amounts of lava and two conspicuous volcanoes stand out on the skyline: the Hengill central volcano (803 m) and the huge lava shield of Skjaldbreiður (1,060 m). Other large eruptive units belong to a group of Pleistocene hyaloclastite mountains like the table mountain Hrafnabjörg, the Kálfstindar Ridge (a multi-peaked tuff-ridge) and the shapely Botnsúlur massif (1,093 m).

■ 100 km of fissures

The Þingvellir area and Hengill belong to one of the four volcanic systems of the Reykjanes Peninsula (Chapter 5); the Hengill Volcanic System. The fissure swarm is approximately 100 km long and cuts through the lava west of the town of Þorlákshöfn at the south coast and continues towards Hengill across the Hellisheiði foothills, where the fissure swarm is crossed by the road between Reykjavík and Hveragerði at Hveradalir. The swarm then furrows across the group of late Pleistocene ridges, hills and peaks which form the Hengill volcanic centre (Fig. 21). Both there and on Hellisheiði numerous volcanic fissures show signs of postglacial (Holocene) activity. Large Holocene lava flows have partly filled the depressions in the older eruptive formations.

The fissure swarm lines the western shore of Lake Þingvallavatn north and northeast of Hengill, and forms, in fact, a part of the lake bed. It then cuts into the slopes of the Skjaldbreiður volcano and reaches into the valley of Kaldidalur.

Apart from the Skjaldbreiður lava shield and a few other similar structures, the recent eruptive units consist of about 10 volcanic fissures lined with spatter or scoria cones. Their total eruptive volume is estimated as 5-6 km^3. The big lava shields, on the other hand, are very voluminous, ranging from 2 to 17 km^3 each.

The Þingvellir area is easily reached by a 50 km-long road from Reykjavík. The down-faulted area has been studied in detail. The results indicate that the graben is slowly widening, but its floor is also sinking, in addition to sudden movements caused by tectonic events. During such events, the graben floor may suddenly subside up to 1 m and earthquakes shake the area. This happened, for example, in 1789.

The horizontal extension in 1967-1979 was 3 mm per year, and the sinking of the central graben floor in 1967-1990 1 mm per year on average.

■ A powerhouse for the Reykjavík area

None of the volcanic fissures southwest of Hengill date from historical times. The group of Hellisheiði lavas (I-IV) seems to include flows which are more than 5,000 years old, to lavas about 1,900 years old. The youngest lava flow was emitted from fissures both southwest and northeast of Hengill itself, as well as from fissures cutting into the mountain massif (Fig. 22). It dates from the first century AD, apparently from a volcano-tectonic episode where discontinuous fissure sections were active during successive events in the system. In the northeast, a 5.5 km-long fissure section then produced the Nesjavallahraun lava (11 km^2). A smaller segment still farther northeast opened up on the bottom of Lake Þingvallavatn and gave rise to Sandey

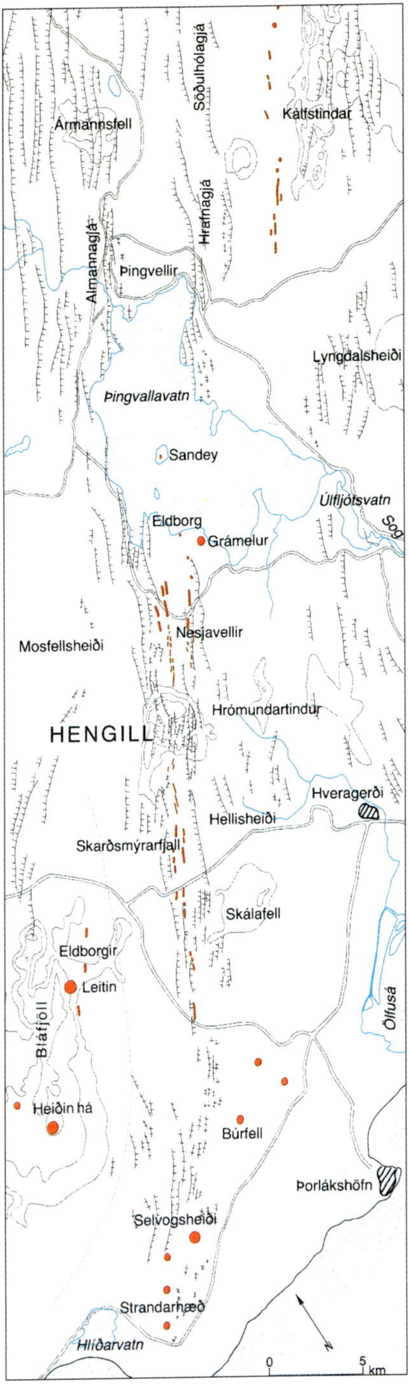

21. *The Hengill Volcanic System, showing tectonic fractures and the main postglacial volcanic fissures (thick lines) and lava shields/craters (dots).*

island by forging two tephra craters into one.

A large magma chamber lurks beneath the central part of Hengill and a smaller one is located near the town of Hveragerði. The interaction between heat from the roots of Hengill and groundwater gives rise to a powerful high-temperature geothermal area. Steaming vents and fuming mud-pots are widely found, and a part of the area, the Nesjavellir Geothermal Field, is now exploited. Steam from boreholes is used to generate electricity and produce hot water for the Reykjavík Municipal Heating Service.

■ The huge shield

The Skjaldbreiður lava shield is located somewhat east of the main fissure swarm. It resembles an upturned soup plate and rises some 600 m above its surroundings. The summit is a lava ridge on the rim of a 300 m-wide lava crater, but the slopes (7-8° incline) consist of wind-polished ropy pahoehoe lava. The crater was the site of a bubbling lava lake, but the molten rock was channelled to the slopes by tube-like caves. Estimates of the volume of lava range from 15 to 17 km^3 and the lot is believed to have been produced in one long-lasting eruption (perhaps 10-20 years) some 9,000-10,000 years ago. Similar but older volcanoes are found southeast (Lyngdalsheiði) and northwest (Ok) of Skjaldbreiður, and also at the far southeastern end of the Hengill fissure swarm. Selvogsheiði, 2.2 km^3, is at least 6,000 years old.

22. The Hengill central volcano: a cluster of diverse volcanic structures, predominantly made of hyaloclastites. Two magma chambers are found within the crust, one beneath the highest part (with snow), the other farther to the east (right). The Nesjavellir geothermal area can be seen in the centre and Lake Þingvallavatn in the background.
(Photo: Oddur Sigurðsson)

The explanation for voluminous effusive eruptions shortly after the recession of the Pleistocene ice caps may partly be found in crustal movements, caused by the receding ice. When the weight of the overlying ice decreases, the plates adjust by rising relatively rapidly. The movement creates stresses in the crust and increases excess magmatic pressure in the reservoirs, enabling magma to surface directly from these deep sources. The majority of recent lava shields date from the first 5,000 years after the last glaciation.

The Skjaldbreiður lava flowed far to the south. It is, however, not seen at Þingvellir or in the fault walls there, because it is largely covered by a younger lava flow. Some 8,000-9,000 years ago, a 15 km-long fissure opened up southeast of Skjaldbreiður and east of Hrafnabjörg (Eldborgir at Tindfjallaheiði). It must have been a grand sight to observe floods of lava gushing from such a long line of vents. The fast-flowing lava eventually covered at least 100 km^2 and solidified into the ropy lava (pahoehoe) seen everywhere at Þingvellir. The Skjaldbreiður and Eldborgir lavas entered the prehistoric Þingvallavatn lake which occupied a basin made by glacial erosion, damming by subglacial eruptions and tectonic movements. The lava flow reduced the lake by half and created a lava dam. The water level rose some

EXAMPLES OF VOLCANIC FISSURES AND LAVA SHIELDS IN THE HENGILL VOLCANIC SYSTEM AND ÞINGVELLIR AREA

Name	Type	Lava km^3/km^2	Remarks
Lambahraun	lava shield	-/-	Approx. 3,000-4,000 years old
Skjaldbreiður	lava shield	17/>200	At the eastern edge of the Hengill swarm – 10,000 years old
Selvogsheiði	lava shield	2.2/50	East of Þorlákshöfn
Eldborg undir Meitlum	crater row	-/-	About 2,000 years old
Reykjafells-sprunga (He IV)	crater row	-/-	From the first century AD,close to Hveradalir
Nesjavalla-sprunga	crater row	-/>10	Same event as He IV. Near power plant
Tjarnarhnúkur	scoria crater		Many thousands of years old, in Hengill
Búrfell	lava shield	0.05/2	Made of picrite
Tindfjalla-heiðar-sprunga (Eldborgir lava)	crater row	-/>100	Fast flowing pahoehoe, seen at Þingvellir

-/- = no data

25 m and the lake spread to about two thirds of its present size. Erosion of the lava dam and slow sinking of the graben floor have since increased the lake to its present size and lowered the water level.

■ Hidden volcanoes and well-known lava caves

There has been no volcanic activity north or east of Lake Þingvallavatn for the past 9,000 years, except for eruptions in the Langjökull area. It is generally suggested that there are two volcanic systems located beneath the 1,000-km^2 Langjökull ice cap. No radio echo soundings have, however, yet been made on the ice cap. A few acid outcrops and scattered postglacial (Holocene) eruptive units or faults are the only indicators of these systems. Volcanic structures include lava shields

23. A lava cave (Surtshellir, approx. 2 km long). Such caves are commonly lava tunnels, channelling red-hot ropy lava (pahoehoe) from a crater during an effusive eruption.
(Photo: Sigurður H. Stefnisson)

like Kjalhraun, the craters of Geitlandshraun (west of the ice cap), and small volcanic fissures north of Langjökull (e.g. Krákshraun lava) and on top of Mt. Hagafell in the south. The most recent eruption occurred when the widespread Hallmundarhraun lava (200 km^2) west of Langjökull flowed in around AD800-900. It contains Iceland's longest lava caves (Kalmannshellir, Surtshellir, Víðgelmir, Fig. 23), structures up to 3,000 m-long. Some are up to dozens of metres wide. The caves are large lava tubes within newly formed lava flows, channelling fluid lava from craters or lava streams into the spreading lava fields. Many such tubes collapse but quite a few prevail as spectacular, winding caves. They may contain vividly coloured chemical deposits and various types of lava dripstones, formed while the lava was still glowing. Most lava caves are found in ropy lava flows (pahoehoe).

A Showcase of Rifting

The Reykjanesskagi peninsula can be regarded the place to observe how the submarine Mid-Atlantic Ridge (Reykjanes Ridge) merges onto the landborn volcanic rift zone of Iceland. There, four volcanic systems straddle the divergent plate boundaries, dotted with fissures, faults, volcanic vents and geothermal fields. Recent lava flows have enlarged the area of Reykjanesskagi by some 1,000 km^2.

■ An important window

The Mid-Atlantic rift segment off the southwest coast of Iceland is called the Reykjanes Ridge. It is made up of small offset ridges containing downfaulted areas (grabens) and volcanic formations. Earthquakes are frequent at the Reykjanes Ridge and written sources suggest at least 12 submarine eruptions off the coast. Most of these eruptions date from the 13th century, but there are also accounts of new islands such as Nýey in 1783 and recent volcanic eruptions in 1830, 1879 and 1884. The older

24. The southwestern tip of the Reykjanes Peninsula, bounded by a graben. The Karlinn sea stack in the foreground dates from a submarine eruption in the 13th century. The dark Stampar yngri lava dates from the same volcanic episode (Reykanes Fires). A high-temperature geothermal area is seen behind the lighthouse. (Photo: Ágúst Guðmundsson)

Eldey Island and some skerries are of fairly recent volcanic origin.

On land, the continuation of the Reykjanes Ridge bisects the boot-shaped Reykjanesskagi (Reykjanes Peninsula, Fig. 24). The rift axis, representing the plate boundaries, bends sharply to the east. The rift zone, containing the axis, consists of four sub-parallel volcanic systems (Fig. 25). Each system comprises low mountains and ridges made of various types of tuff and breccia (hyaloclastites) or pillow-lava. Furthermore, open fissures, normal faults, crater rows and small to medium-sized lava shields, as well as geothermal fields, are found within each volcanic system. Even though this spreading-ridge section is somewhat different from the submarine one, it offers a unique opportunity to study the structures and processes which characterize the spreading ridges of the world. Reykjanesskagi is a kind of a window where we can look into processes which generally occur hidden from our sight.

■ A recent addition

The Reykjanes Peninsula is geologically young. To the east and north there are 2-4-million-year-old rocks, but the peninsula bedrock is younger than 700,000 years. The Quaternary Ice Age

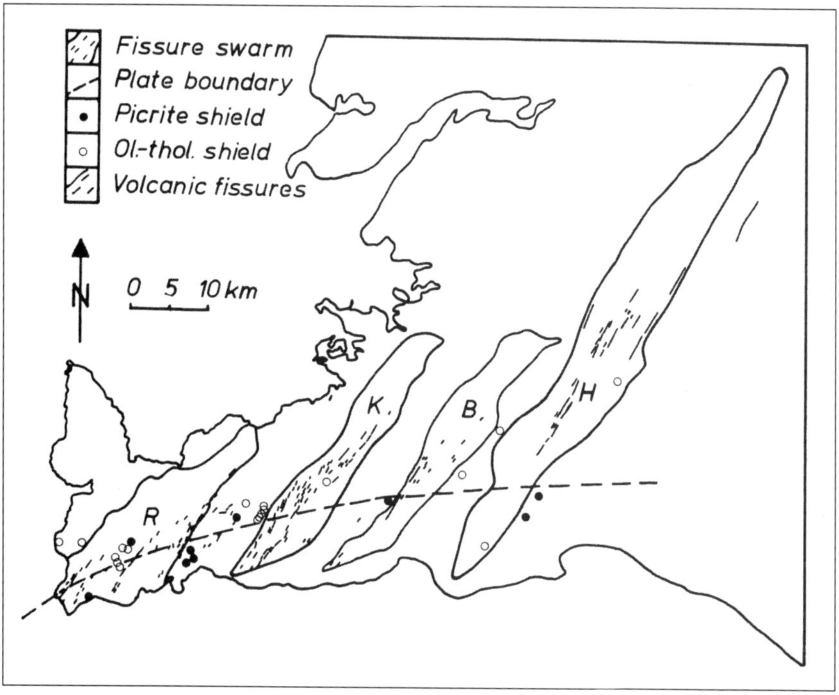

25. The four volcanic systems of the Reykjanes Peninsula (from left to right): Reykjanes Volcanic System, Krísuvík (or Trölladyngja) Volcanic System, Brennisteinsfjöll Volcanic System and Hengill Volcanic System. The plate boundaries are shown with a stippled line. Volcanic fissures and lava shields are presented, along with the Hengill volcanic centre (H).

26. A typical volcanic fissure with a crater row on the Reykjanes Peninsula (near Djúpavatn lake). The fissure and the associated moss-grown lava flow were formed during the Krísuvík Fires in the 12th century. (Photo: Oddur Sigurðsson)

(Pleistocene) began in Iceland approximately 3 million years ago. Consequently, the rocks on the Reykjanes Peninsula span several glacial and interglacial periods of the late Pleistocene. The part of the bedrock from the glacial periods consists of the above-mentioned hyaloclastites, pillow-lava and glacial sediments or sediments from rivers, lakes and the sea. The part of the bedrock from the interglacials consists mainly of scoured basaltic lava flows.

The hyaloclastites are volcanic eruptives, formed in an environment with abundant ice or water. Most of these rocks date from glacial periods when the area was covered by ice caps. In coastal areas some formations may have originated in the sea during times of receding ice. Among the most prominent subglacial volcanic structures are table mountains (stapis). They are very common in Iceland and occur as barrel-shaped piles of hyaloclastites and pillow-lava capped with a small lava flow. Table mountains are thought to pile up in cavities formed by subglacial eruptions, as are the long, serrated tuff ridges widely seen on Reykjanesskagi and within or near the active volcanic zone (see Chapter 6).

The Reykjanes Peninsula became ice-free some 12-13,000 years ago. More than 40 km^3 of eruptive rocks have been added to the landmass during the past 10,000 years (postglacial time or Holocene). About 200 volcanic fissures (some are in fact contemporary fissure segments) and single vents have enlarged its area by approximately 1,000 km^2.

■ Four active volcanic systems

The bent plate boundaries intersect with each of the four volcanic systems on the peninsula. They, however, line up (NE-SW-trending) in a subparallel fashion due to the crustal tension. The westernmost one is the Reykjanes Volcanic System (Fig. 14). It is a well-known source of earthquakes but has not developed a prominent volcanic centre. There are, on the other hand, some 40 postglacial (Holocene) eruptive fissures (crater rows) in the system, as well as 14 lava shields, including olivine-rich and primitive picrite lavas. The associated fissure swarm has a very marked downfaulted northeastern

EXAMPLES OF VOLCANIC FISSURE ERUPTIONS AND LAVA SHIELDS ON THE REYKJANES PENINSULA

Name	Type	Lava km^3/km^2	Remarks
Stampar yngri	crater row	-/ 4.6	5 km fissure dating from 1226 also submarine craters
Eldborg undir Geitahlíð	crater row	-/ 11	main crater is a large spatter cone
Heiðin há	lava shield	6.8/170	largest of its kind in the area
Þráinsskjöldur	lava shield	5.2/130	easily seen from the Reykjavík-Keflavík road
Leitin	lava shield	>3.0/130	dating from 2600BC - lava entered Reykjavík
Eldborgir	crater row	0.24/12	Svínahraun lava from AD1000
Búrfell	scoria/spatter cone	-/-	about 7,000 years old lava entered the town of Hafnarfjörður
Eldborg við Drottningu	crater row	-/-	a lava ring at the road to Bláfjöll Ski Centre
Sandey	large scoria cone	-/-	an island in Lake Þingvallavatn dating from the first century AD part of a volcanic event in Hengill
Ögmundarhraun	crater row	0.13/16	a part of a volcanic episode AD1151-1158

-/- = no data

27. A group of four maars (early Holocene) near Krísuvík on the Reykjanes Peninsula. Lake Grænavatn (right) has a distinct colour due to sulphur compounds in the water. Geothermally altered hyaloclastites in the background. (Photo: Oddur Sigurðsson)

part (graben) at Vogar. The volcanic system, including the fissure swarm, is 45 km long and up to 10 km wide.

The second system, the Trölladyngja Volcanic System, is 40 km long and 7-8 km wide. The fissure swarm has no central volcano, but 40-50 postglacial (Holocene) volcanic fissures, lined with craters, are found there, as well as 3 lava shields. Its southwestern end is in the vicinity of the town of Grindavík, but the northeastern end cuts partly into the outskirts of Reykjavík.

The third system, the Brennisteinsfjöll Volcanic System, covers the Bláfjöll mountain range and is of similar size as the first. It contains 40 postglacial (Holocene) eruptive fissures and 2 lava shields but no apparent centre.

The fourth and easternmost system, the Hengill Volcanic System, is the largest of them all and named after the Hengill central volcano (see Chapter 4). The fissure swarm is 100 km long and up to 15 km wide, containing at least 10 postglacial (Holocene) volcanic fissures. Large shield volcanoes are close by.

■ Many historical eruptions

All 30 Holocene lava shields on the Reykjanes Peninsula are older than 4,500 years. Most of the small ones are made of primitive, olivine-rich picrite lava from deep mantle (reservoir) sources (e.g. Háleyjarbunga). The large ones are made of olivine tholeiites with volumes of up to 5-7 km^3, and their ropy lava flows (pahoehoe) cover 100-170 km^2. Examples are Heiðin há and Þráinsskjöldur.

The crater rows are mostly of the spatter- and scoria-cone type (Fig. 26). A few maars are also present (Fig. 27). The eruptive volumes from the fissures amount to 0.1-0.4 km^3 and, correspondingly, the scoria-type lava flows (aa) have typical areas of 5 to 35 km^2.

Although eruptions are scarcely mentioned in contemporary written sources, some 12-15 lava fields on the Reykjanes Peninsula prove to be from historical times. Some represent individual volcano-tectonic events within a single volcano-tectonic episode. Modern methods of dating show that the oldest of the lava flows, from the 10th or 11th century, are found in Bláfjöll and Heiðmörk (10-15 km east of Reykjavík), in Brennisteinsfjöll and close to the main road between Keflavík and Reykjavík (Afstapahraun). Among early 11th-century lava flows is the one mentioned in the old Sagas in reference to the adoption of Christianity in Iceland in AD1000. It has been identified as the Svínahraun lava (or Kristnitökuhraun) cut by the main road between Reykjavík and Hveragerði.

Two prominent volcano-tectonic episodes occurred on the Reykjanes Peninsula between 1151 and 1188, and in 1211-1240. During the former (Krísuvík Fires in the Trölladyngja Volcanic System), discontinuous fissures opened up, nearly 25 km long, and emitted many lava flows (0.22 km^3 and 36 km^2). Among them are Ögmundarhraun (in 1151) east of Grindavík, and Kapelluhraun at Straumsvík. Ruins of a farm are found within the Ögmundarhraun lava flow. The latter episode (Reykjanes Fires in the Reykjanes Volcanic System) produced some 6 lava flows including Stampahraun yngra (in 1226) near the tip of Reykjanes, and the Illahraun lava at the Blue Lagoon. The source of the so-called Medieval Layer was a submarine phreatic eruption at Reykjanes, around 1226. The rock pinnacle Karlinn is a remaining part of a big tephra crater at the coast, forming the southwestern proximity of the Stampar yngri crater row.

The last burst of volcanic activity occurred in the 14th century in the Brennisteinsfjöll volcanic system. Then the Selvogshraun lava flowed around 1340.

After more than 600 years of inactivity, however, the probability of a new volcanic eruption in one of the Reykjanesskagi volcanic systems in the near future increases as each year passes.

It seems, however, that the eruptions on land in historical times are rather small, each episode only producing a few tens of square kilometres of lava. The main danger for the populated areas in the Southwest may then lie in the fact that roads, powerlines, freshwater supply systems, heating power plants and skiing areas are found within the four volcanic systems. Towns like Grindavík and Hafnarfjörður are partly built on recent lava flows, indicating that populated areas could be endangered by nearby eruptions.

March 2021

Related but Different

The steep and shapely Herðubreið and the flat, symmetrical cone of Kollóttadyngja in Northeast Iceland represent two characteristic volcanic formations: the subglacially formed stapis (table mountains or tuyas with lots of tuff) from the Ice Age and the recent lava shields (made of thin lava flows). Both types and tuff ridges related to the stapis are found all over the rift zone in Iceland.

■ Of similar breed

Within or close to the present active volcanic zone one readily notices large, circular and isolated mountains of volcanic origin. Usually, they rise hundreds of metres above their surroundings and many bear little resemblance to the classic cone-shaped volcanoes which people picture in their minds.

One group of these mountains is the lava shields, already mentioned in previous chapters; for example, Skjaldbreiður. The steeper shields (5-9° flanks) may surely be related to volcanic activity because of their symmetrical shape (Fig. 28). Flat lava shields appear almost as plateaus and do not always seem to be of volcanic origin (1-3° flanks).

Each lava shield originates in a long effusive eruption which produces only fast-flowing ropy lava (pahoehoe), often very widespread.

28. The Trölladyngja lava shield (1,460 m), like Kollóttadyngja, is one of the largest volcanoes of this type in Iceland. At least 7,000 years old, it rises 600 m above the surroundings and the top crater measures 1,200 m across. (Photo: Ágúst Guðmundsson)

Another group, including at least 40 large mountains, comprises bulky, barrel-shaped and flat-topped mountains called table mountains or tuyas (sing. stapi in Icelandic). They consist of many tuff layers, breccia (termed hyaloclastites together) and thick formations of pillow-lava. Such eruptives resemble a stack of round, jointed lava lumps. The flat mountain-tops may be covered with lava (Fig. 29) or with a small ice cap on top of the lava (Fig. 30).

The third group includes ridge-shaped mountains or chains of rugged peaks (made of hyaloclastites), some of which may be cone-shaped with debris-covered slopes, the tuff-ridges (Fig. 21).

Hrútfell (1,390 m, Fig. 30)) west of the Kjalvegur mountain track, Herðubreið (1,678 m, Fig. 29) in the northeast and the nearby Kollóttadyngja (1,177 m) are all well-known mountains. The first two fall in the group of table mountains but Kollóttadyngja and Trölladyngja (Fig. 28) in the first, being lava shields. The Jarlhettur mountains south of Langjökull ice cap are a typical tuff-ridge.

All these mountains are volcanic structures, but why are they so different from stratovolcanoes and crater rows, both regarding their shape and the appearance of the eruptives (which are all, in fact, basalts)?

■ Ice or no ice

The answer lies in the environmental

29. The Herðubreið table mountain (stapi, 1,682 m), NE-Iceland. The mountain is thought to have been formed during one prolonged eruption within the ice cap of the last glacial period of the Quaternary Ice Age. It is made of palagonite tuff and breccia (hyaloclastites), capped with a small lava shield. (Photo: Halldór Kjartansson)

30. Hrútfell (1,390 m), central Iceland; a glaciated table mountain (stapi), probably from the last glacial period of the Ice Age. (Photo: Ari Trausti Guðmundsson)

conditions at the Earth's surface during volcanic eruptions. It has been observed that submarine eruptions produce the same type of eruptives as are found in Icelandic tuff-ridges and in the table mountains. These structures can be traced back to relatively large volcanic eruptions of very fluid basalt beneath ice caps, especially during the glacial periods of the Pleistocene. In the absence of ice (or meltwater) the eruptions, on the other hand, give rise to lava shields and lava flows. The ice, however, creates special conditions leading to the formation of table mountains (very short fissures) or the multi-peaked tuff-ridges (long fissures). Each peak on such ridges then represents a subglacial volcanic vent.

■ Ice meets fire

When a subglacial eruption occurs on a short fissure beneath an ice cap, the magma meets an ice sheet which is at least hundreds of metres thick (up to 1,000-2,000 m). High water and ice pressure and rapid cooling by meltwater lead to pillow-lava formation. (Fig. 31) A water-filled dome forms in the ice until water escapes and flows under the adjoining ice. At that stage decreasing water and ice pressure make pillows break up due to contraction by cooling and internal gas pressure in the pillow-lava. A breccia-type mixture of pillow-bits and glassy, tephra-like material then caps the heap of pillow-lava, and the dome can still expand. The cavity turns into a large hole in the ice cap, which is subsequently filled by layers (Fig. 33)

31. Pillow lava. It forms from basaltic lava in contact with water under some pressure; beneath glacier ice, in lakes or in the sea. Above: The pillow lava is overlain by palagonite-tephra (tuff) from the phreatic phase. Individual pillow, radially jointed and with a glassy crust. (Photos: Halldór Kjartansson)

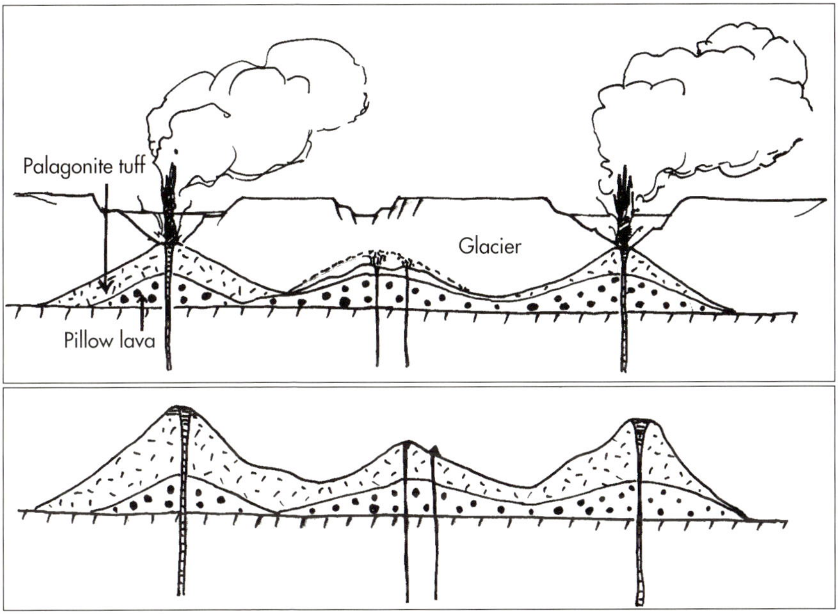

32. Tuff ridges (hyaloclastite ridges) are remnants of subglacial fissure eruptions. Each cone is an independent volcanic vent. Víðidalsfjöll, NE-Iceland. The drawing is a schematic representation of this type of volcanic event.
(Photo: Halldór Kjartansson, drawing: Ari Trausti Guðmundsson)

from a visible and explosive tephra eruption. The tephra is granulated magma from a vent or vents submerged in water.

The glass in the tephra is altered with time by heat and water and the tephra-grains are cemented together by mineral deposits (palagonitization). If the eruption stops before any lava is emitted, a tuff cone is formed (such as Keilir on the Reykjanes Peninsula). In the case of a long fissure, most eruptions come to an end at this stage, producing the above-mentioned ridges or chains of hyaloclastite and pillow-lava peaks; the tuff-ridges. (Fig. 32)

An eruption may continue beyond this stage, usually on a short fissure. In that case, lava flows freely over the tephra deposits as soon as water no longer meets magma in the volcanic vent. A small lava shield is formed, the very top of a table mountain. Herðu-

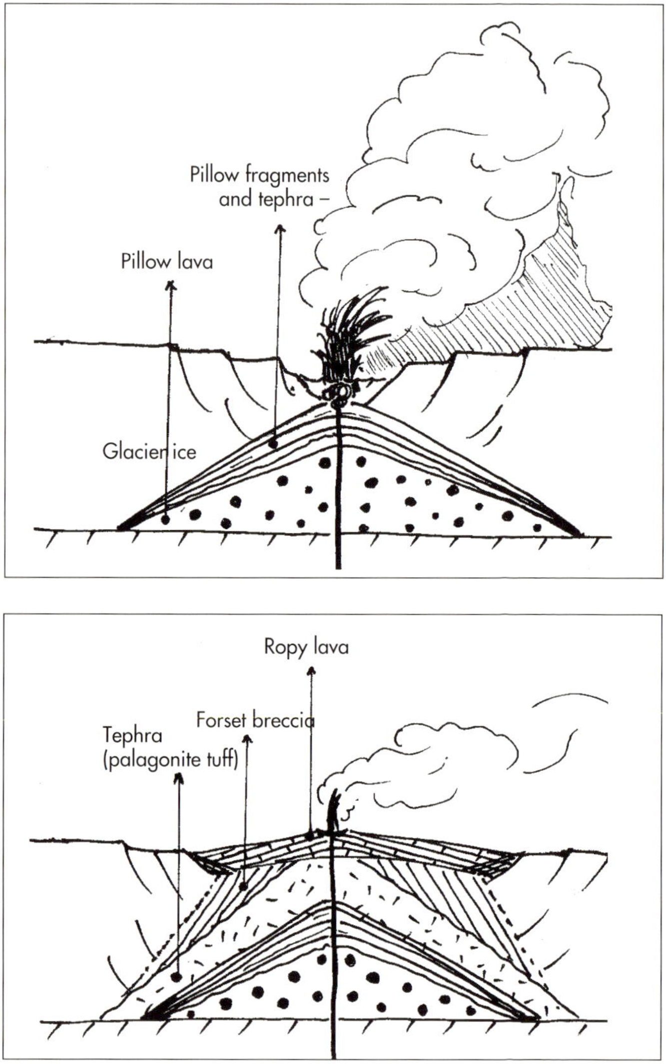

33. A schematic representation of the two last stages of a subglacial (or in some cases, a submarine) eruption. If an eruption stops prior to the effusive, final stage, a tuff-cone is preserved (e.g. Keilir, Reykjanesskagi). The final stage allows a lava cap to form on top of the volcanic structure, to be revealed as a table mountain (stapi) when the glacier recedes (e.g. Herðubreið, NE-Iceland). (Drawing: Ari Trausti Guðmundsson)

breið's top crater and lava cap are evidence of this final stage (Fig. 33).

Thus, Herðubreið (or Hrútfell) and Kollóttadyngja (or Trölladyngja) are indeed sisters of the same breed, but from different environments: the two table mountains probably rose in the ice sheets of the last glacial period which started 120,000 years ago, while the lava shield dates from the present rather warm, period (interglacial?), only a few thousand years old. New petrological data indicates that there are substantial chemical variations in the Herðubreið rocks. That, in turn, could indicate that there may be rock units of different age in the mountain, something which is hard to reconcile with the theory of each table mountain being formed in one prolonged subglacial eruption.

7. THE HOFSJÖKULL VOLCANO

The Hidden Giant

Until recently, the huge caldera and volcano hidden under the ice blanket of the Hofsjökull ice cap were unknown features of the volcanic zone in Iceland. This remote area has now been explored and details of the volcano and its associated volcanic formations are now available. The volcanic history, however, is still rather obscure.

■ The third largest ice cap

An almost circular ice cap reaches a dominating altitude of 1,800 m in the central highlands. Some 22 outlet glaciers flow in all directions and a few rocky outcrops (nunataks) protrude from the highest regions of the ice cap. It is called Hofsjökull and was hardly ever investigated until the 1970's.

Hofsjökull has an area of 925 km^2, measures 40-50 km across, and is up to 750 m thick but around 200-250 m on average. The ice volume is 208 km^3.

The Hofsjökull ice cap is located within the neovolcanic zone, east of the slightly larger Langjökull ice cap. Only a few Holocene craters or lava flows are found near the margins of Hofsjökull and it was not known for a long time what kind of volcanic structures were hidden under the ice cover, if any at all (Fig. 34).

34. A large Icelandic ice cap: Hofsjökull. The 925-km^2 ice cap covers a large central volcano with a caldera. Some 4-5 postglacial lava flows are found in the vicinity.
(Photo: Ari Trausti Guðmundsson)

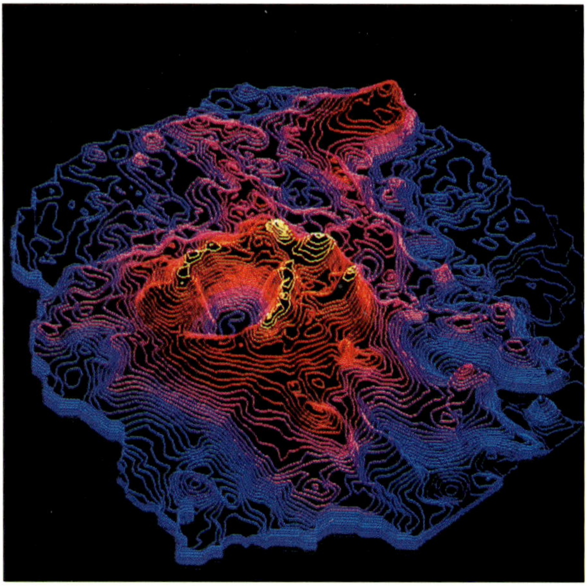

35. The Hofsjökull central volcano as revealed by radio echo soundings. The prominent mountain with a 750-m-deep caldera is seen in the centre.

■ Revealing soundings

In 1973 a satellite photo (ERTS-1) showed a distinct but shallow depression in the top dome of the Hofsjökull ice cap. It was interpreted as evidence of a caldera structure beneath the ice. Ten years later scientists used a radio echo depth-measuring device to obtain a picture of the landscape hidden under the ice. It became evident that a bulky and craggy 1,500-1,600 m-high dormant volcano lay under the frozen beds of Hofsjökull. It has an area of 200 km^2 at the 1,000-m elevation contour and holds a 750 m-deep and 8 km-wide (70 km^2) ice-filled caldera (Fig. 35). Two mountain ridges are connected to the volcano and most of the nunataks (e.g.

36. Tungnafellsjökull is a glaciated central volcano including a small caldera. The volcanic activity in the Holocene (for the past 10,000 years) is very limited.

(Photo: Ari Trausti Guðmundsson)

37. The Kerlingarfjöll mountain massif southwest of the Hofsjökull ice cap. These colourful rhyolite mountains may be an individual volcanic centre.
(Photo: Ari Trausti Guðmundsson)

Hásteinar) are simply ice-free parts of the caldera rim, made of rhyolitic rocks.

■ An unknown history

No written records, known tephra layers or any other evidence of subglacial, Holocene eruptions in Hofsjökull have been found. The volcanic history of the big Hofsjökull central volcano is unknown. There are, however, at least 4 different, recent, postglacial (Holocene) lava flows close by and, if joined as eruptive units to the centre, a 30-40 km-long and 20 km-wide volcanic system can be defined at Hofsjökull. The best-known lava is the Illahraun lava, northeast of the rhyolitic Kerlingarfjöll mountains (Fig. 26). They show, on the other hand, some characteristics of an individual volcanic centre. It is also possible that this rhyolitic massif, with its vigorous geothermal activity and small flank glaciers, may be associated directly with the Hofsjökull volcano.

East of Hofsjökull is a small independent volcanic system with a central volcano, Tungnafellsjökull (1,520 m), and an associated caldera, partly filled by an ice cap. (Fig. 36) Two inconspicuous Holocene eruptive fissures are found northeast of the volcano.

Central volcanoes become as much as 1.5-2.5 million years old. The Hofsjökull volcano has a high and little-eroded profile. It seems to be a rather young structure, which is also indicated by recent nearby lava flows. This may imply that the giant in the ice cap is almost certainly a slumbering volcano. If it awakes, the volcanic eruption could be a very powerful one. On the other hand, another thousand years are only a trifle on the geological timescale.

The Outsiders

A small volcanic system is located in Southern Iceland, somewhat isolated from its next neighbours of the same kind. It is now a very popular area for outdoor activities and dotted with hundreds of summer cottages. The present craters and lava flows date from one volcanic episode some 6,000 years ago making people speculate on future unrest in the area.

■ A densely populated area

North of the town of Selfoss and east of the spring-fed Sog River lies the region of Grímsnes. It is characterized by rather rough scoria lava (aa), grown over with lush birch woods and dotted with reddish scoria and spatter cones. Several farms are scattered through the region and many hundred summer cottages form individual colonies. During the summer thousands of people visit the area, enjoying the fine surroundings.

Viewed as a whole, most of the Grímsnes region forms a small volcanic system well east of the much larger Hengill volcanic system (Chapter 4). The Grímsnes Volcanic System is only 12 km long and 4-5 km wide, the smallest in Iceland. It is located at the border of the main rift zone or, if viewed in terms of size and distance from the Hengill Volcanic System, strictly outside the rift zone. The Holocene Grímsnes basalt lavas are, however, of the tholeiitic series which is characteristic of the fissure swarms within the rift zone.

■ The fire - fountain episode

There are 12 eruptive units to be found in the Grímsnes region. Most volcanic fissures are 400-800 m long, with 2-4 craters. Four very short fissures, however, gave rise to only one scoria cone

ERUPTIVE UNITS IN THE GRÍMSNES VOLCANIC SYSTEM

Name	Number of craters	Fissure m	Lava flow km^2
Selhóll nyrðri	3	400	3.5
Rauðhóll	2	400	>1.0
Borgarhólar	1	–	0.4
Kálfshólar	2	800	8.0
Seyðishólar-Kerhóll	2	>800	23.5
Tjarnarhólar	4	800	11.9
Selhóll syðri	1	–	–
Rauðhólar	3	300	–
Álftarhóll	1	–	6.2
Kolgrafarhóll	1	–	–

38. The well-known Kerið crater in Grímsnes. Kerið may be a typical explosion crater (maar), but as no ejecta has been found the alternative explanation of a collapsed scoria crater has been put forward. (Photo: Kjartan Halldórsson)

each. The lava from all the fissures covers 54 km^2.

Research indicates that all the fissures opened up within a time-span of a few centuries 5,000-6,000 years ago. The second eruption (event) in the series (volcanic period or episode) was the largest one. The big craters Seyðishólar (Fig. 39), Kerhóll and Tjarnarhólar are brightly coloured red hills north and south of the Grímsnes road. During this event, magnificent lava fountains must have shot into the air because both Seyðishólar and Kerhóll are high hills made of lots of scoria and lava bombs. This second eruption in the series produced 100 million m^3 of tephra and the lava covered an area of about 35 km^2, with overlapping, individual lava flows.

The best-known crater from the Seyðishólar-Tjarnarhólar eruption is Kerið, located a few hundred metres south of the Grímsnes road. It is a 55 m-deep pit (the opening is 270 m long and 170 m wide) with a deep-blue pond which is about 10 m deep (Fig. 38). Since long ago Kerið has been regarded as an explosion crater (maar), but no traces of the ejecta have been found. An alternative explanation is that it is a collapsed scoria crater.

■ Why is it there?

This small volcanic system might be explained as a newly born fissure system, associated with the Reykjanes Rift Zone (which runs between Reykjanes and Langjökull). If so, many volcanic-tectonic episodes could follow the first

39. The Seyðishólar and Kerhóll craters (upper middle) from the Grímsnes Fires episode some 6,000 years ago. A part of the same volcanic fissure with the Kerið crater is seen to the right of the road. (Photo: Oddur Sigurðsson)

one. Another possibility relates to the South Iceland Seismic Zone, a transverse fracture zone in the southern lowlands. It is the location of many large earthquakes and runs to the east at a 50-60° angle to the Grímsnes fissures. It extends approximately between the town of Hveragerði and the Hekla volcano. The volcanic activity in Grímsnes might be related to the stress field generated where this fracture zone meets the rift zone. It has been suggested that the fracture zone moves very slowly to the south. In that case the volcanic activity in Grímsnes might be temporary, even a one-time phenomenon. Further volcanic unrest could then be expected farther south. Lava bombs from Seyðishólar contain bits of plutonic rocks and drillings have revealed an intrusive body beneath the Grímsnes area. Maybe there is more to the volcanic history of Grímsnes than is known today.

The Long Fire Fissure

A cluster of lava shields akin to the big Hawaiian volcanoes, pit craters and a discontinuous 70 km-long volcanic fissure are among the features of two volcanic systems in the Northeast of Iceland. The centres of both systems were once sites of important sulphur mines.

■ Two lesser volcanic systems

The Askja and Krafla Volcanic Systems are the most conspicuous ones in the rift zone in Northeast Iceland.

There are, however, two other systems present in this zone; the Fremrinámur and Þeistareykir Volcanic Systems. The former is squeezed in between the Askja and Krafla fissure swarms but the latter has the northernmost position of them all. Neither system has developed a typical postglacial central volcano. Instead, large lava shields, geothermal activity and small outcrops of acid eruptive rocks indicate possible, slow-developing centres.

■ The Þeistareykir fissure swarm

The Þeistareykir fissure swarm cuts through postglacial (Holocene) lava flows northwest of Lake Mývatn. It is 60 km long and 5-10 km wide. A clus-

40. The central parts of the Þeistareykir Volcanic System include the lava shield of Þeistareykjabunga (with snow). Faults and lava flow from the recent Krafla Fires in the foreground. (Photo: Oddur Sigurðsson)

ter of Pleistocene (Ice Age) mountains and a group of lava shields form an elevated central part which, supposedly, covers an old volcanic centre.

Þeistareykir is a geothermal field. Two large, interconnected lava shields, Þeistareykjabunga (564 m) and Stóravítisdyngja (551 m), both with large summit craters, are approximately 10,000 years old, along with other smaller tholeiitic eruptive units (Fig. 40).

A few postglacial eruptive fissures are found within the fissure swarm belonging to the Þeistareykir Volcanic System. Among the youngest is the one which produced the Bóndhólshraun lava, west of the Gæsafjöll table mountain, about 5,000 years ago.

The most recent volcanic eruption in the Þeistareykir area occurred in a complex lava shield northwest of Bæjarfjall Mountain. The lava flow is called Þeistareykjahraun and seems to be approximately 2,500-3,500 years old.

Most lava fields in the vicinity of the lava shields are characterized by deep pits, some of which were formed when roofs of subterranean lava channels collapsed (termed pit craters). The most noted is Víti at Stóravítisdyngja.

■ The Fremrinámur Volcanic System

A 120 km-long fissure swarm extends from the Ketildyngja lava shield southeast of Lake Mývatn to the sea at the Melrakkaslétta peninsula. If the Fremrinámur geothermal field at Ketildyngja is a central feature of the swarm, it has practically no southern section. The developing volcanic centre is, in that case, close to a cluster of two large lava shields (Ketildyngja, 939 m, and Kerlingardyngja, 986 m) and two smaller ones. The Ketildyngja shield is about 3,000-4,000 years old and a few postglacial (Holocene) eruptive fissures are found in the central area. The Ketildyngja lava (Laxárhraun eldra) entered the Mývatn area and reached, prior to the Laxárhraun yngra lava from Lúdents- and Þrengslaborgir, the shores of the bay of Skjálfandaflói.

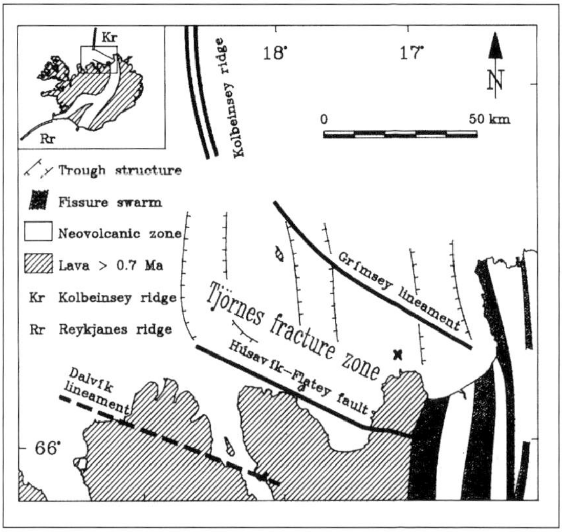

41. The Tjörnes Fracture Zone lies between the Northeast Iceland Rift Zone (right) and a rift zone segment of the Mid-Atlantic Ridge called the Kolbeinsey Ridge. Submarine trough structures, strike-slip faults (trending NW or WNW), normal faults (trending N) and NW-trending seismic lineaments characterize the fracture zone. Submarine volcanic eruptions have occurred e.g. at Mánáreyjar (marked x).

42. The river Jökulsá á Fjöllum cuts the graben of Sveinar and Randarhólar. Note the crater-row, partly within and outside the graben. (Photo: Oddur Sigurðsson)

The main volcanic fissures are, however, the Kræðuborgir crater row and the Sveinar crater row (the latter with different names for various individual segments).

Kræðuborgir are large scoria and spatter cones on a 10 km-long fissure, flanked by still longer faults. The lava flow, called Búrfellshraun, is 2,500-3,000 years old and the youngest eruptive unit in the Fremrinámur volcanic system.

The Sveinar row (Fig. 41) is one of the longest volcanic fissures in Iceland. It stretches, as a discontinuous row of small and large scoria and spatter cones, for 70 km. Rauðuborgir are the southernmost craters, followed by Sveinar (near the "ring-road"), then Ytrisveinar and Randarhólar. Between Ytrisveinar and Randarhólar the river Jökulsá á Fjöllum plunges over the Dettifoss waterfall into the magnificent canyon of Jökulsárgljúfur (a national park). Farther north are Rauðhólar and Kvensöðull craters, and finally the

43. The Hljóðaklettar formations are strangley shaped lava plugs, remains of craters and thick lava flows from early Holocene times. The „Echo Cliffs" were eroded by the nearby glacial river Jökulsá á Fjöllum. (Photo: Halldór Kjartansson)

northernmost craters, which are also called Rauðhólar (at Melrakkaslétta). Many faults flank the crater row, forming one or more grabens. The volcanic fissure may have opened up step-wise during a rifting event. It is believed to be 6,000-8,000 years old.

West of the middle segment of the Sveinar fissure, there is another volcanic fissure that was active shortly before the Sveinar fissure erupted. It is an oblique, 6 km-long fissure, called the Rauðhólar fissure, located in the Svínadalur valley and at Hljóðaklettar in the Jökulsárgljúfur National Park. Glacier bursts in Jökulsá á Fjöllum and river erosion have cleared most of the lava flow away, as well as the tephra from most of the craters. The renowned and interesting Hljóðaklettar pinnacles are the remaining crater plugs, made of jointed and columnar basalt (Fig. 43).

■ Off-shore volcanism

The Tjörnes Fracture Zone extends from the bay of Öxarfjörður, northwest to the submarine Kolbeinsey Ridge rift zone. It is bordered by at least two large transform faults, the Grímsey fault and the Húsavík-Flatey fault. The zone itself is characterized by 3 or 4 north-south-trending trough structures. The main crustal movements in this basic type of ocean-ridge discontinuity occur in the transform valley associated with the Húsavík-Flatey fault (Fig. 42). Strike-slip movements are common, along with the associated earthquakes. No volacnic activity has been registerd in this part of the fracture zone. This is, however, the case within the NW-trending trough structures closer to the Grímsey fault. There are a few reports of, or references to, volcanic eruptions in the region. Some may have occurred on the Kolbeinsey ridge but others within the fracture zone, as indicated by references from 1372 and 1755. The former mentions an island north of the inhabited island of Grímsey. The only truly reliable source on an eruption in the area, however, is the journal, Norðanfari, in 1867. It tells of earthquakes and an eruption north of the small islands of Mánáreyjar off the Tjörnes peninsula.

10. KATLA

The Wicked Witch

Katla is one of the most violent central volcanoes in Iceland. Named after a wicked witch in the Icelandic folklore, it encompasses the largest caldera in Iceland, 110 km². The volcano also produces the most fearful jökulhlaups (glacier bursts, floods) in Iceland discharging at least 100,000-200,000 m³ of water per second. The last one rushed across Mýrdalssandur in 1918 and now the volcano is long overdue in relation to its average time of repose (47 years).

■ The tale of the wicked woman

There is a story in the large collection of Icelandic folktales concerning the notorious volcano Katla, located beneath the ice cap of Mýrdalsjökull (580 km², 130 km³) in Southern Iceland. The story tells of a wicked female cook in the monastery of Þykkvabæjarklaustur. She had magic trousers enabling her to run fast and without a break. When she discovered that a shepherd had misused her priceless belongings, she killed him and hid in a big barrel of whey. When confronted with the revelation of her crime as the whey was slowly being used up, she fled in the trousers up to the mountains and flung herself into a dark crevasse in

44. Mýrdalsjökull ice cap. An aerial view of the upper region of the ice cap, covering the large caldera of the Katla volcano. (Photo: Ari Trausti Guðmundsson)

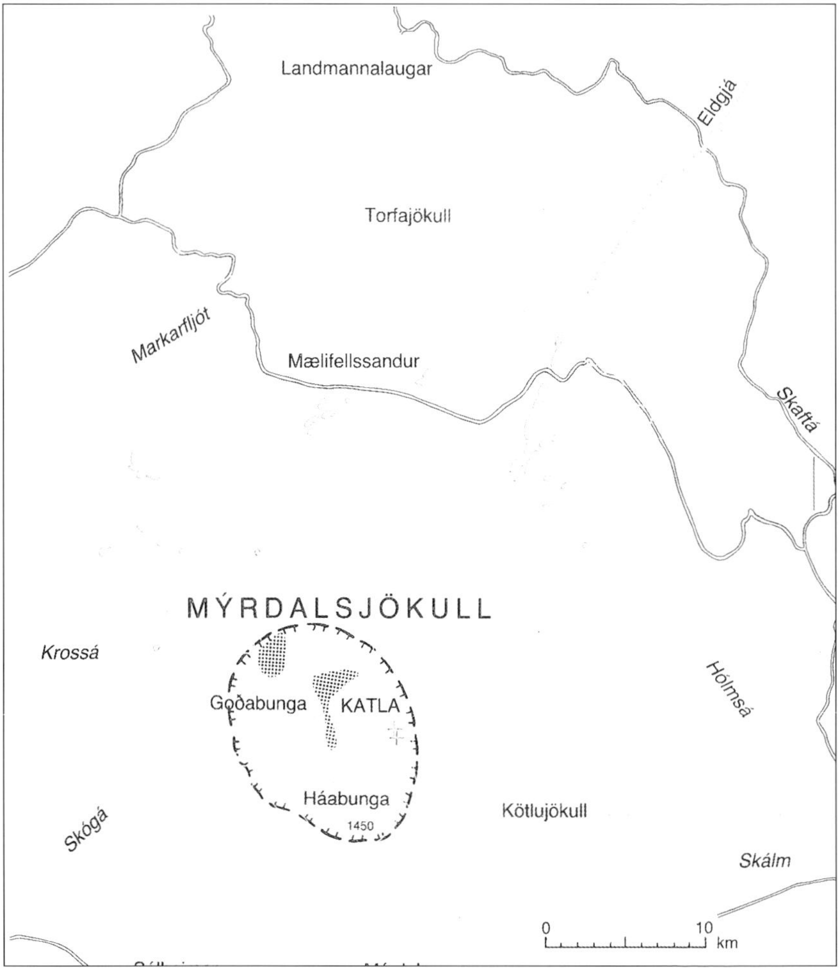

45. The Katla Volcanic System. The approximate caldera outlines are shown as well as volcanic craters or fissures (dots and thick lines). + denotes the eruption site in 1918.

the ice cap. Ever since, according to tales, she avenges her fate by pouring fire and water onto the nearby regions.

Today we know that a large volcanic centre lurks beneath the 200- to 750-m-thick ice cover of Mýrdalsjökull (Fig. 44). The volcano has developed a 600- to 700-m-deep caldera with an area of 110 km^2. It is the largest of its kind in Iceland. In addition, there are numerous volcanic fissures flanking the northwestern and northeastern sides of the ice cap. The most prominent one is a 40 km-long chasm called Eldgjá (Fig. 48). Eldgjá is up to 400 m wide and 150 m deep in places.

■ Iceland's largest caldera

The ice cap conceals a large 1,400 m-high mountain massif. For a long time little was known about the landscape below the frozen blanket, but new radio echo soundings have now revealed the structures beneath the ice cap. Apart from the caldera rims, there are distinct hills on the caldera floor and elsewhere and three deep passes cut through the rims, made by glaciers. These are: Kötlujökull pass (900-1,000 m above sea level), Entujökull pass (1,000-1,100 m above sea level) and Sólheimajökull pass (950-1,050 m above sea level).

Seismic research indicates that there is a lens-like magma chamber beneath the caldera, at the depth of maybe only 1-2 km! It may be 1-2 km deep and up to 3 km long or 12-24 km^3, but underneath it a large plutonic body may exist, as indicated by a strong positive gravity anomaly.

Seismic activity is very lively at Katla. There is, for example, a long record of intense earthquake swarms in the autumn, in two distinct centres; one beneath the eastern part of the caldera floor, the other beneath the ice dome of Goðabunga, west of the caldera. The earthquakes may be related to the deloading of the thin crust above the chamber due to summer melting of the ice cap each year and to high groundwater pressure in the caldera roof at the same time.

There are more than 30 craters and crater rows in the Katla Volcanic System. The largest one, the Eldgjá fissure, indicates forceful volcanic activity. Smaller volcanic fissures (craters or crater rows) are located northeast, north and northwest of the ice cap. Together with the Katla central volcano, the fissures form an 80 km-long and up to 20 km-wide volcanic system (Fig. 45). Up to 100 eruptions have occurred there during the past 10,000 years, producing 30-35 km^3 of tephra (mainly from Katla) and 15 km^3 of lava (mainly from the historical Eldgjá Fires and the Hólmsár Fires, about 6600 BP, before present). The eruptive material is predominantly basaltic magma which belongs to the transitional series. The Katla eruptions produce tephra only because of the encounter between the ascending magma and lots of meltwater. At least 11 Holocene eruptions, however, in 6400-1700 BP, produced acid tephra. Prior to that, a catastrophic eruption occurred in Katla, indicated by thick ignimbrite layers in Mýrdalur and by deposits (Z1 – Ash Zone 1) found on the ocean floor hundreds of kilometres south of Iceland. This explosive eruption, 10,600 BP, produced probably more than 10 km^3 of tephra which spread to an area between Labrador and Norway. It may also have caused much of the caldera subsidence in Katla.

All in all, Katla is a large and vigorous volcano, along with its satellites, and seemingly the most productive volcanic system in Iceland, whereas Hekla is the most productive single volcano.

■ At least 20 historical eruptions

In historical times at least 20 tephra eruptions penetrated the ice cap of Mýrdalsjökull (Fig. 79). The first two might have been as early as around AD900 and 920. The third occurred in AD934. At that time, Eldgjá also opened up, as a part of a discontinuous volcanic fissure, stretching 75 km to the northeast of Katla. There is conclusive evidence that this 10th-century volcanic episode was very productive. Up to 20 bursts of activity (volcanic events) may have occurred on the Eldgjá fissure. Some 4 km^3 of tephra (as dense rock) were erupted and maybe as much as

10 km^3 (700 km^2) of lava flowed southwards from Eldgjá, seen for example in Álftaver. Emissions from other large and old crater rows near Eldgjá might, however, have created some of the enormous lava field between the eastern Mýrdalssandur and eastern Landbrot, which would then be, at least in part, over 5,000 years old.

Some of the later Katla eruptions were destructive, large tephra eruptions, especially the two in the 18th century. The eruption in 1755 spewed out 1.5 km^3 of tephra. The smallest Katla eruptions only produce 0.02 km^3 of tephra. A small glacier burst in 1955 may have been triggered by a subglacial volcanic eruption.

The last major eruption took place in 1918 and lasted 24 days (Fig. 46). It penetrated 400 m-thick ice in the eastern part of the caldera. The eruption cloud (mostly steam and tephra) rose 14 km in the air and fierce lightnings were very common. Tephra fell over thousands of square kilometres. The volume is estimated as 0.7 km^3 (700 million m^3). As the average time of inactivity between eruptions is about 47 years, Katla is long overdue. Since this is a fearsome volcano, seismometers are used to monitor the volcano and, if possible, to warn of an imminent eruption. Tiltmeters and GPS-measurements have also been applied.

■ Huge torrents of water, ice and sand

The need to monitor Katla and the fearsome reputation of the volcano stem from the fact that each eruption is followed by a catastrophic meltwater flood: a glacier burst (jökulhlaup in Icelandic). Very rapid melting of ice by magma produces water and mud flows which are usually released only a few hours after each eruption is noticed. The glacier bursts are sudden and short-lived but their volume may be in excess of 1,000,000,000 m^3 (1 km^3).

All the subglacial caldera-rim passes, mentioned above, are potential waterways for glacier bursts. Of these, 15 historical ones have passed the Kötlujökull pass, onto Mýrdalssandur, and 2 bursts crossed the Sólheimajökull pass, onto Skóga- and Sólheimasandur (13th century). Some 1,600 years ago, a glacier burst passed the Entujökull pass and at least 6 bursts flowed across the Sólheimajökull pass 2,000-4,000 years ago.

Most historical Katla glacier bursts flood large parts of a 600 km^2 Mýrdalssandur wasteland east of Mýrdalsjökull only 2-3 hours after an eruption penetrates the ice. Prior to that a water-filled dome probably expands in the ice cap, because the eruption does not pierce the ice at once. With increasing water pressure the water is released from under the Kötlujökull glacier with tremendous force, forming swift, broad torrents of an incredibly muddy and dense liquid. The torrents flush gigantic blocks of ice to the sea and the sediment builds up flats, extending the beach line many kilometres farther out. Estimates of the flood discharge range between 100,000 and 300,000 m^3 per second and the velocity at least 20-50 km per hour! Usually, the floods diminish in a matter of days, and their total volume during each eruption varies with the rate of magma discharge and the duration of the volcanic event.

The black torrents of Katla have laid waste large amounts of fertile land and destroyed dozens of settlements.

At present, Katla endangers not only

46. The mushroom-shaped steam and tephra cloud over Katla in 1918, seen from the surroundings of Vík. (Photo: Kjartan Guðmundsson)

ERUPTIONS OF KATLA IN HISTORICAL TIMES

Year	Tephra km³	Duration days
*900	–	–
*920	–	–
*934	–	–
11th century	–	–
*1179	–	–
1245	–	–
1262	–	–
*1357	–	–
1416	–	–
15th century	–	–
(possibly twice)	–	–
*1500	–	–
1580	–	–
1612	–	–
1625	–	13
1660	–	>60
1721	–	>100
1755	1.5	120
1823	–	28
1860	–	20
1918	0.7	24

* = uncertain

a few scattered farms or communities close to Mýrdalssandur or Skóga- and Sólheimasandur but also the small village of Vík. The sandy strip of land now existing between the beach at Vík and the cliffs east and north of the village consists entirely of deposits from Katla's bursts. Flood waves could sweep towards the village within a few hours after the outbreak of an eruption. Evacuation plans exist and the seismic monitoring of Katla may ensure that they would be carried out, as well as enabling the main road along the southern coast to be closed for traffic.

At present, there are, however, no trustworthy indications of when "the wicked witch" might disturb people again.

48. Eldgjá is defined as a mixture of a volcanic and tectonic fissure, set with tephra and lava craters. Eldgjá proper is 40 km long, but the active fissure during the forceful eruption in AD934 seems to have been up to 70 km long. A view to the Northeast.
(Photo: Ragnar Th. Sigurðsson)

11. EYJAFJALLAJÖKULL

The Quiet One - until 2010

The onset of a series of earthquakes located in the Eyjafjallajökull stratovolcano on the south coast in 1994 reminded Icelanders that the mountain must be regarded as an active volcano. So does its recent eruption of 1821–1823. The mountain rises some 1,666 m above the main road and dozens of farms and is renowned for its scenic beauty.

■ An icy mountain

Not many summits of glaciated volcanoes on Earth are accessible by car. The Eyjafjallajökull mountain (1,666 m) in Southern Iceland is, by using a powerful 4-wheel-drive vehicle fitted with over-sized, partly deflated tires. The route crosses an 80 km^2, crevassed glacier from the west to one of the small peaks, rising from the rim of a 2.5 km-wide top-crater. A very steep ice-fall (Gígjökull) plunges from the crater almost to sea level, into a small lagoon below the northern flank of Eyjafjallajökull (Fig. 49).

The Eyjafjallajökull stratovolcano,

49. Eyjafjallajökull (1,666 m), an active stratovolcano at the south coast. The 2.5-km-wide top crater is filled with ice and a glacier (Gígjökull) descends into a small marginal lake.
(Photo: Ari Trausti Guðmundsson)

50. The Tindfjallajökull massif is a volcanic centre with an old caldera, seen here from the southeast. (Photo: Ágúst Guðmundsson)

the centre of the Eyjafjallajökull Volcanic System, is easily spotted from vast distances in the Southern Lowlands. It belongs to the South Iceland Volcanic Zone (Eastern Volcanic Zone) which is characterized by big volcanic centres of a similar type or calderas. The mountain is one of Iceland's highest and a shapely one indeed.

■ Only two historical eruptions?

The bulk of Eyjafjallajökull is younger than 700,000 years. Much of it consists of different, large formations of either hyaloclastites from glacial periods or lavas from interglacial periods of the late Pleistocene. The rocks range from dacite (acid rock) to basaltic ankaramite, all belonging to the transitional series.

For the past 13,000 years, however, the volcanic activity seems to have been at a low key. In the 30 km-long and 8 km-wide fissure swarm which traverses the entire mountain and the ridges to the east, only 3 or 4 postglacial (Holocene) sites of eruptions can be traced (Fig. 53). Two fissures produced the Hamragarðahraun and Kambagilshraun lava flows on the ice-free western flank of the mountain many thousands of years ago (Fig. 51). A subglacial summit fissure, however, was the site of the only certain historical eruption, in 1821-1823. The tephra production was luckily moderate, considering the large farming districts close to the mountain. Neither were the meltwater floods of any great proportions. An eruption of Eyjafjallajökull in 1612 is mentioned in one of the old annals. Other sources only describe an eruption in Katla in 1612. No conclusive evidence of a contemperaneous event in Eyjafjallajökull exists.

The notorious Katla volcano, east of Eyjafjallajökull, woke up as Eyjafjallajökull ceased activity in 1823 (supposedly also in 1612), indicating a "mechanical link" of some sort between the neighbouring giants. These two volcanoes are, all the same, individual centres, as seen, for example, by the distinctly different chemical composition of their eruptive rocks.

■ A volcano with a past

Facing Eyjafjallajökull in the north is a multi-summited mountain massif. A small ice cap is located on its northern flanks but seen from the air, a clear-cut caldera encircles the two highest peaks (Ýmir, 1,462 m, and Ýma) which are both made of acid rocks. This is the Tindfjallajökull massif, an old volcanic centre (Fig. 50).

A few scoria craters and the glaciated centre form the small Tindfjallajökull Volcanic System. The scoria craters and the associated fissure eruptions seem to date from early postglacial times, but there are no indications of any activity for thousands of years. The volcanic system is, however, considered an active one as quiescent periods of up to many thousands of years are well known from volcanic centres.

The Tindfjallajökull caldera formation could be associated with a very powerful explosive eruption some 200,000 years ago. A thick layer of fused tephra and airborne rock fragments (pyroclastics) is found south of the volcano, buried under younger formations. This ignimbrite is, for example, found in the popular Þórsmörk area.

51. The Seljalandsfoss waterfall. A much-loved sight by travellers, the waterfall plunges across a resistant step made of lava (Hamragarðahraun) from an eruptive fissure high up on the Eyjafjallajökull volcano. (Photo: Ragnar Th. Sigurðsson)

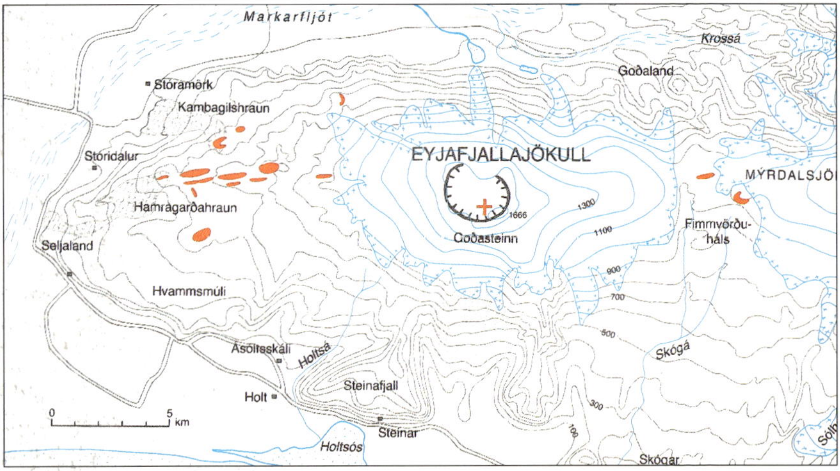

52. A map of the glaciated Eyjafjallajökull volcano. The cross and the semicircle denote the large summit crater (or a small caldera). Thick, short lines and spots are eruptive fissures or individual scoria craters younger than 10,000-13,000 years.

The Astronauts' Training Ground

During the 60s, American astronauts heading for the Moon were trained for geological research. One of their objectives in Iceland was the big and remote Askja caldera in the Dyngjufjöll mountains. Its interesting volcanic history includes a powerful plinian eruption in the caldera and many distant fissure eruptions in the 1880s, a series of lava eruptions from fissures in the 1920s and an instructive effusive fissure eruption in 1961, producing pahoehoe lava.

■ A triple caldera

The most conspicuous caldera in Iceland (Askja) is located in the middle of a 1,500 m-high mountain massif, Dyngjufjöll, in central Northeast Iceland. The bulky central volcano, largely made of hyaloclastites, is completely ice-free. Therefore, three differently aged calderas are easily recognizable. They are rimmed by 200-400 m-high scarps and their floors covered with lava flows. Together the

53. The short, but initially powerful, fissure eruption in Askja 1961.
(Photo: Guðmundur Einarsson)

54. Askja central volcano has a triple caldera structure; the main caldera with a smaller one, cradling Lake Öskjuvatn (dating from 1875) and the northeastern, older caldera. The total caldera area is 45 km². A view towards Mt. Herðubreið (left)
(Photo: Ingibjörg Kaldal)

calderas form a 45 km^2 structure which is associated with a large fissure swarm (Fig. 55).

The Dyngjufjöll central volcano rises from a big cluster of lava fields called Ódáðahraun (meaning the Lava of Evil Deeds). It constitutes the largest and most desolate continuous lava desert in Iceland. Much of Ódáðahraun is tholeiitic basalt lava flows from at least 10 small and large lava shields in the area. The big Trölladyngja (1,460 m), Kollóttadyngja (1,177 m) and Ketildyngja (986 m) each produced large fields of ropy lava (pahoehoe) flows which have now been scoured by drifting sand and are practically devoid of vegetation. A few of the lava flows from the Askja Volcanic System are included in Ódáðahraun.

The first generation of American lunar astronauts did some of their train-

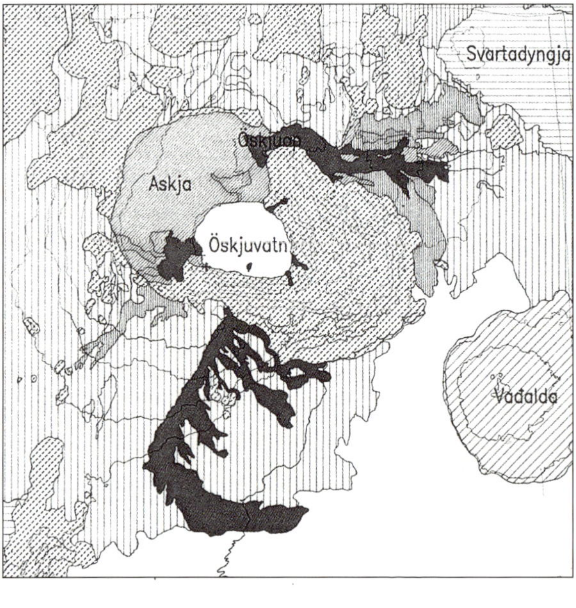

55. The Dyngjufjöll volcanic centre. Slanting lines: fissure lavas, dating from 2800 BP to AD1470, mainly on the caldera floor (Askja). Stipled, slanting lines: hyaloclastites (Pleistocene), forming the main Dyngjufjöll massif. Dark shading: fissure lavas, dating from 1920-1961. Older lavas not presented and no volcanic or tectonic fissures shown.

ing in this area, including Neil Armstrong, who was the first human to set foot on the Moon.

■ An active past

Pleistocene volcanic rocks constitute the bulk of the Dyngjufjöll massif. The large-volume lava eruptions producing lava shields within and close to the volcanic system are older than 4,500 years. These eruptions and others, producing substantial volumes of tephra, may have influenced the main caldera collapse (Fig. 54). The lava production prior to 4,500 BP is at least 20-30 times higher than in the period from 2900 BP to the present time. This has been attributed to intense volcanism as the Ice Age glaciers were melting in the early Holocene (decreasing lithostatic pressure and lively crustal movements due to rapid isostatic rebound).

Rifting processes have formed a 140 km-long fissure swarm. Its section south of Dyngjufjöll is short, but the section north of Dyngjufjöll is very long. Faults and grabens stretch far across Northeastern Iceland.

Many crater rows occur both inside and outside the Askja caldera. In some cases magma has been injected into the crust from a magma chamber beneath Askja and reached the surface, but in other cases the magma may have ascended from a deeper (8-12 km), and larger, magma reservoir, more or less underlying the whole volcanic system.

Some 40 Holocene eruptive fissures are known in the Askja Volcanic System, but only a few of the associated lava flows or tephra layers are actually dated. The lava volume since 2,900 BP is only 0.95 km^3. The historical record is poorly established but it seems that at least a 400-year period of quiescence elapsed until a vigorous volcano-tectonic episode made its impact in 1874-1876.

RECORDED ERUPTIONS IN THE ASKJA VOLCANIC SYSTEM

Date	Location	Eruptives	Remarks
Jan. 1875	Askja and fissure swarm	Uncertain (lava?)	Only seen from afar
Feb. 1875	West of Sveina-gjá	Basaltic lava	Fissure eruption
March 1875	West of Sveina-gjá and in Sveina-gjá	Lava, many km^2	Eruptions from fissures
March 1875	Askja (SE part)	Acid tephra 2.5 km^3	Two very short eruptions
April1875	Near and in Sveinagjá	Lava, many km^2	Eruptions and from fissures
July 1875	Fjallagjá	Lava	
Aug. 1875	Sveinagjá	Lava	
Oct. 1875	Sveinagjá	Lava	Probably end of episode
There are uncertain references to eruptions in Sveinagjá in 1876			
March 1921	Near Víti, Askja	Lava, 0.3 km^2	Bátshraun lava
Nov. 1922	West of Öskju-vatn	Lava, 2.2 km^2	Mývetninga-hraun lava
Dec. 1922	SE of Öskjuvatn	Lava	Kvíslahraun lava
Feb. 1923	SE of Öskjuvatn	Lava, 1 km^2	Suðurbotna-hraun lava
1926	Öskjuvatn	Tephra 0.05 km^3	An island formed
1924-1929	South of Askja	Lava, many km^2	References to eruptions until 1933
Oct.-Nov. 1961	NE part of Askja	Lava, 0.1 km^2 Tephra, 0.004 km^3	Vikrahraun lava

■ Fire fountains and tephra blasts

Some unrest in Dyngjufjöll was noticed by people in of Northeast Iceland in 1874. In February that year, earthquakes and new steam columns seen above Dyngjufjöll indicated the beginning of tectonic events. They continued almost the whole year through. The first volcanic eruption in the Askja Volcanic System started in January 1875; a basaltic lava-producing fissure eruption northeast (or south) of Askja, along with an eruption in Askja proper. In February, more fissure eruptions occurred, this time in or close to the Sveinagjá graben (40-70 km north of Askja). More such volcano-tectonic events followed in March, and in the closing days of that month a tremendous two-phase eruption occurred in Askja. New volcanic vents blew out 2.0-2.5 km^3 (0.5 km^3 as dense rock) of light-coloured tephra (dacite) in two main short bursts during a two-day eruption. Most of the tephra fell in East and Northeast Iceland, turning daylight into almost complete darkness. The rapid expulsion of magma from the magma chamber caused a part of the chamber-roof to collapse. An 11 km^2 caldera gradually developed within the main caldera floor. The new depression was subsequently filled with groundwater, forming Iceland's deepest lake (Öskjuvatn, 220 m, Fig. 54).

Fissure eruptions, producing more basaltic lava flows, commenced after the big blast in Askja, in or near the Sveinagjá graben, until late 1875 or early 1876 and produced a total of 29 km^2 (0.3 km^3) of basaltic lava flows (Nýjahraun lava).

The course of events indicate a volcano-tectonic rifting episode which started before the big eruption in Askja and continued after it. The episode consisted of 10-11 eruptions and numerous tectonic events. A sudden rush of basaltic magma from the deep-seated reservoir into Askja's magma chamber, which contains acid magma in its upper part may have triggered the explosive event in Askja, as well as having supplied magma to the faraway Sveinagjá fissures. Other mechanisms are also possible, such as rifting of the caldera roof and lateral magma injections from lower parts of the chamber, generating blade-like dykes.

■ The 20th-century eruptions

Volcanic events continued into the 20th century, about 40 years after the last of the Sveinagjá events. At least 8 fissure eruptions occurred in Askja in 1921-1929 (or as late as 1933). Four small lava flows appeared near to the new caldera lake (1921, 1922 and 1923), and a volcanic island formed in the lake itself (1926). Somewhat larger fissure eruptions also took place during a volcano-tectonic rifting episode south of the caldera in 1924-1929 (1933), producing more fluid basalt lava flows than the other fissures (about 0.3 km^3).

Then, in 1961, a new volcanic fissure (Vikraborgir) opened up on a ring fracture, near the northeastern edge of the main Askja caldera. High basaltic lava fountains spouted for two months (Fig. 69). The lava volume is almost 100 million m^3 and the tephra volume is 4 million m^3. The pitch-black basalt (tholeiite) covers 11 km^2.

■ More to come?

Precise geodetic measurements in Askja show that the caldera floor is subsiding. These movements, as well as frequent small earthquakes, point towards magma on the move deep down in the crust. The recent volcanic history indicates somewhat frequent eruptions, even if most are small. Other tell-tale signs, like changing geothermal activity in Askja, tell us that further volcanic activity in the volcanic system may be expected within a relatively short time-span.

The Queen of Volcanoes

Of all the Icelandic volcanoes, one is well-known the world over: Hekla. The mountain has erupted 20 times in historical times and produced more eruptive material for the past 8,000 years than any other active volcano in Iceland. Still fuming, its last eruption occurred in 1991 and lasted for 53 days. A large magma chamber or reservoir has been found beneath the mountain and its associated volcanic system.

■ Iceland's most productive volcano

Set in the background of the Southern Lowlands, Hekla (1,480 m) is a grand mountain. From the south it resembles a cone-shaped stratovolcano, but reveals the shape of an upturned boat when viewed from the east or west. White firn and a small glacier high on the northwestern slopes appear as a white blanket on broad shoulders, lending a name to this long feared and awesome volcano (Fig. 56). Hekla means a knitted shawl, but the name could have another root.

Hekla was once thought to be one of the entrances to Hell and described with fearful respect in medieval literature. In modern times, Hekla is probably Iceland's most famous volcano. The mountain certainly has caused severe damage to land, crops and farms in his-

56. Hekla (1,480 m), Iceland's most famous volcano, seen from the southwest. The mountain is ridge-shaped, mostly of postglacial age and very active. The river Ytri-Rangá in the foreground. (Photo: Ágúst Guðmundsson)

57. The eruption of Hekla in 1947. This was a powerful event in the beginning, with a eruption cloud rising to 20-25 km and an initial phase producing tephra and lava. The volume of eruptives became 1 km³ in 13 months. (Photo: Vigfús Sigurgeirsson)

torical times, but very little is known about loss of life due to these eruptions.

Seventeen historical eruptions have been recorded in the mountain itself and at least an additional five in the Hekla Volcanic System. The average period of inactivity is 55 years. Most of the eruptions of Hekla proper occur in a 5.5 km-long summit fissure with numerous craters. They produce both tephra (sometimes acid) and andesitic lava flows (Fig. 58). The fissure eruptions outside the mountain, however, produce basaltic tephra and lava flows. Added together, the volume of the eruptive rocks from the transitional series, produced during the past 10,000 years, is almost 33 km³, of which tephra is 7.2 km³. In historical times Hekla has added almost 10 km³ of volcanic products to Iceland (7 km³ if calculated as dense lava), thus becoming the country's most productive central volcano.

■ ... the bottomless pit of Hell...

Hekla is mentioned in early writings, such as Liber miraculorum from Clairvaux (AD 1180) and always as a fearful and awesome entrance to the Devil's dungeons, until the Age of Enlightenment in the 18th century. It was climbed in 1750 by the Icelandic explorers Eggert Ólafsson and Bjarni Pálsson and their findings added to the scientific approach of understanding the true nature of Hekla.

Hekla is located at the western margin of the South Iceland Volcanic Zone (Eastern Volcanic Zone). The composite ridge seems to be a fairly young formation which is probably growing to become a typical stratovolcano. Its base includes hyaloclastites of late Pleistocene age, but the many tephra layers and lava flows are younger than 8,000-9,000 years.

There are indications of a typical large magma chamber or rather a reservoir at a depth of 6-8 km (probably 5 km wide and 7 km deep) beneath the Hekla Volcanic System. The bulk of the chamber or reservoir contains basaltic magma. There, chemical and physical processes such as partial melting and assimilation of crustal rocks, crystal fractionation and mixing can occur. They induce a layered (or zoned) magma content, with acid and intermediate magma at the top of the magma store but basalts at deeper levels. Long periods of inactivity between eruptions lead to eruptions of lightweight, acid magma in Hekla, from the chamber's or reservoir's top sections. Consequently, the eruptions are more explosive and produce a lot of tephra after such long dormant periods. The mechanisms in the magma chamber or reservoir also give rise to abundant andesitic (intermediate) magma. Thus, after an explosive start, the Hekla eruptions usually produce andesitic lavas, which in turn become more and more

58. Slow-moving scoria lava (aa) margin during the Hekla eruption of 1980.
(Photo: Ágúst Guðmundsson)

59. The southwestern end of the active fissure on the crest of Hekla in 1991 in the first night. The steep angle sustained fast-flowing lava. (Photo: Ari Trausti Guðmundsson)

basaltic during prolonged eruptions. The fissures outside Hekla always produce basaltic eruptives from lower parts of the chamber or reservoir since the acid and intermediate magmas occupy the higher middle sections.

Hekla and associated fissures combined with hyaloclastite ridges form a 40 km-long and 7 km-wide volcanic system. East of it, there is a high-production area or volcanic system, centred around the Vatnafjöll and Rauðfossafjöll massifs with 30 Holocene volcanic fissures. It may be connected to the Hekla central volcano and seen as a flank outcrop of the Hekla Volcanic System or it could be a completely independent system, even associated with the Torfajökull Volcanic System farther east.

■ Distinct phases

At least three phases seem to divide Hekla's volcanic history into different patterns of behaviour. Prior to the formation of the main Hekla ridge, there were numerous fissure eruptions in the Hekla region.

The second phase began with an explosive tephra eruption some 6,000-7,000 BP (H5), followed by another one 4,500 BP (H4). The latter event may have resulted in the formation of a caldera which was filled with eruptives during the subsequent millenniums. Regardless of a possible caldera, at least a substantial mountain was already existing when a tremendous tephra eruption occurred 2,900 BP. About 12 km^3 of whitish pumice (3 km^3 if calculated as dense rock) was blown over

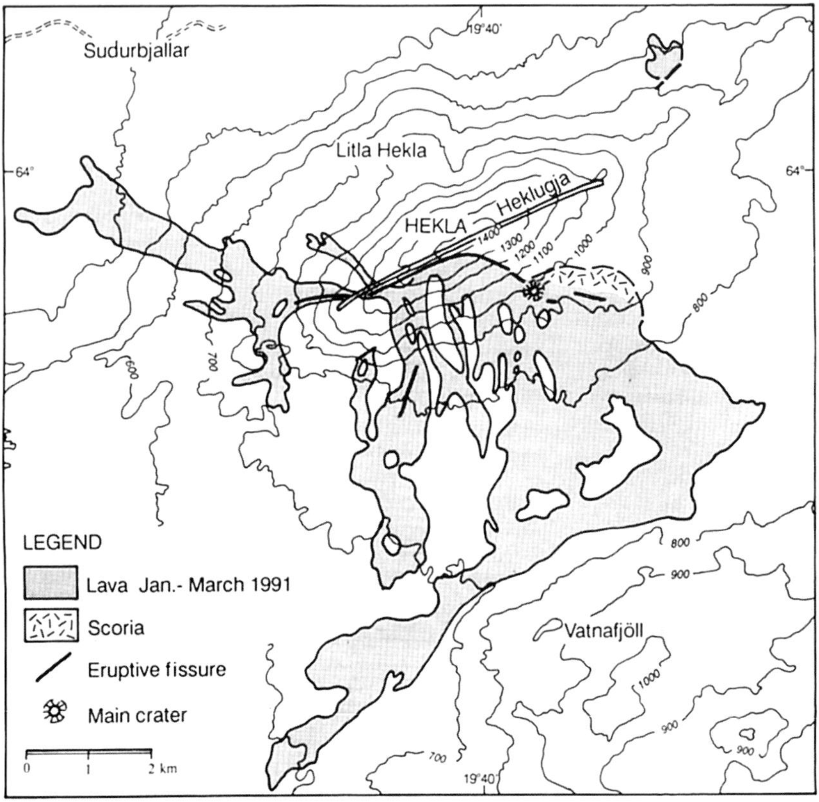

60. The 1991 lava flow from Hekla. Heklugjá is the 5 km-long main fissure on the crest of the mountain, set with craters: the site of the eruption in 1947-1948. In 1970, 1980/81 and in 1991, fissures opened up on the crest, on the flanks and at the foot of the mountain.

80% of Iceland, enough to cover the whole country with a 10 cm-thick layer (H3), if evenly distributed. The final, large eruption in this "tephra phase" caused havoc in populated areas close to Hekla in AD1104, destroying farms and fertile land. Sometime prior to that event, the mixed eruptive activity (producing both lava and tephra) was already initiated, indicated by at least 6 prehistoric but not voluminous tephra layers. These are 1,800 to 2,900 years old but any associated lava flows have been covered by younger ones.

The third phase, devoid of the large tephra eruptions and characterized by mixed eruptions, was finally entered in the 12th century. During the next 8 centuries, Hekla seems to have erupted at least once or twice each century. These eruptions produced substantial amounts of tephra and large lava flows: 0.1 to 1.3 km^3 covering up to 50-100 km^2. At least 7 of the eruptions caused considerable damage to pastures, etc., mainly due to the initial tephra falls.

A hint of a fourth phase with a different eruption pattern may be seen in the 20th century.

■ A new phase?

After the Hekla eruption of 1845 and a fissure eruption in 1878 (the Nýjahraun lava), activity in the Hekla Volcanic System did not resume until 1913. A small basaltic fissure eruption was noticed northeast of Hekla (at Lambafell and Mundafit). Then Hekla spouted fiercely in 1947. The eruption lasted 13 months and produced almost 800 million m^3 of lava (40 km^2) and 210 million m^3 of tephra (Fig. 57). The finest dust was blown 15-20 km in the air and carried by high-altitude winds all the way to Scandinavia.

In 1970 a short but lively eruption occurred on the flanks of Hekla; another one astounded many people in 1980 (Fig. 38), this time in the summit region. One year later Hekla stirred again with a very sudden and short burst of activity.

Yet one more eruption, in early 1991, was just as surprising (Fig. 54). With an initial production rate of 2,000 m^3 a second from many fissures, radiating from the summit, the eruption was an impressive sight. Seismometers recorded earthquakes only 20 minutes before the eruption and there was no imminent warning of it. Observations show that the magma rose from its source with a velocity of 15 km per hour. The eruption lasted 53 days and became confined to one flank-crater for weeks (Fig. 60). The total area of the lava is 24 km^2 (0.15 km^3 or 150 million m^3). The volume of airborne tephra is 22 million m^3, the smallest known, and the tephra sector has an area of 21,000 km^2.

The three latest and rather short eruptions of Hekla, at 10-year intervals, could indicate a new cycle or phase of eruptions characterized by more frequent eruptions than before, and by short fissures opening up on the flanks of the mountain. This could be the effect of changes in the stress field around the magma chamber or reservoir. These changes might be attributed to the propagating rift east of Hekla and the increasing weight of the volcanic rocks, forming the mountain. Repeated eruptions on fissures radiating from the summit would reshape Hekla as a true stratovolcano.

ERUPTIONS OF HEKLA IN HISTORICAL TIMES

Year	Lava km^3	Tephra km^3	Main tephra-sector direction
1104	none	2.5	N
1158	>0.15	unknown	SSE
1206	unknown	0.03	ENE
1222	unknown	0.01	E
1300	>0.5	0.5	N
1341	unknown	0.08*	WNW
1389	>0.2	0.08*	SSE
1510	unknown	0.32	SW
1597	unknown	0.24	SE
1636	unknown	0.08*	NE
1693	unknown	0.3	NNW
1766	1.3	0.4	N
1845	0.63	0.28	SE
1947	0.8	0.21	S
1970	0.2	0.07	NNW
1980	0.15	0.09	N
1981	0.15	0.09	N
1991	0.15	0.02	NNE

* uncertain

The Coloured Hills

Vivid colours and a maze of valleys, gullies and ravines characterize the old and broad volcanic centre of Torfajökull in the southern highlands. One can scramble across obsidian lavas and study geothermal fields, altered rocks and series of differently evolved eruptive rocks. The area includes the famous tourist attraction of Landmannalaugar.

■ Nature's canvas

Iceland is renowned for many strangely shaped and colourful mountains. They are probably nowhere as widespread and eye-catching as in the Torfajökull area (Fig. 62), notably in Landmannalaugar and Jökulgil. Located in the Southern Highlands, the region is visited by several thousand tourists each summer.

The coloured hills owe their existence to the volcanic activity in the area and to the multi-coloured appearance of rhyolitic volcanic rocks. They range from white, yellow, peach and light-red to green, grey and pitch-black (obsidian).

The Torfajökull area is, in fact, a large mountain massif (900-1,270 m), topped by numerous firn-fields and two

61. The subglacially formed Brennisteinsalda mountain, made of rhyolitic rocks. Note the mounds at the volcanic vents which emitted the viscous, acid Laugahraun lava in AD1480.
(Photo: Ari Trausti Guðmundsson)

62. The Torfajökull volcanic centre. Left: a bent ridge from a subglacial eruption (ring dyke). Centre: the Landmannalaugar and Bláhnúkur area. Upper right corner: the Torfajökull ice cap. (Photo: Oddur Sigurðsson)

small ice caps (Torfajökull and Kaldaklofsjökull). The massif contains an old central volcano cut by a 30 km-long and 6 km-wide fissure swarm and constitutes the Torfajökull Volcanic System. The nearby Vatnafjöll high-production area (or volcanic system) is commonly associated with the Hekla Volcanic System but could be linked to the Torfajökull Volcanic System, at least topographically. The postglacial eruptive production of Vatnajökull is 5-10 km^3 (30 eruptive units).

■ An old caldera?

Most of the 400 km^2 area consisting of rhyolitic rocks at Torfajökull accumulated during the late Pleistocene. The largest formation (Jökulgil-formation) is 65,000-115,000 years old. A very voluminous tephra eruption may have occurred in Torfajökull some 65,000 years ago.

Individual eruptive units around Torfajökull comprise differently shaped and coloured mountains. An example is Bláhnúkur (10,000-65,000 years old), located close to the visitors' centre and the natural baths in Landmannalaugar. It is a green and greyish pile of rhyolite with outcrops of pitchstone (or perlite). Close by is Brennisteinsalda, a yellow and reddish ridge, also made of subglacially erupted acid rocks, often shrouded in steam from the geothermal field at its foot (Fig. 61).

The area is characterized by dozens of ridges and peaks, cut by numerous gullies and valleys. The slopes are covered with multi-coloured screes with strange columns, spires and protruding dykes. In this maze of formations a vague outline of a big caldera has been traced, but its existence is disputed. Approximately 20 postglacial (Holocene) eruptive units, however, are easily recognizable as black lavas. They are thought to have originated in 5-10 fissure eruptions, of which two are historical (around AD871 and 1480). The thick and acid Laugahraun lava, towering above the Landmannalaugar baths, dates from the younger event. The volcanic vents, seen as mounds of black, thick lava, are located at the shoulder of the small Brennisteinsalda mountain.

Among the older but Holocene (postglacial) eruptive units are the Hrafntinnusker formation and the impressive craters close to Mt. Laufafell south of the Torfajökull massif. A popular hiking trail, Laugavegur, passes Hrafntinnusker (1,100 m) where large quantities of obsidian are scattered around this mound of thick acid lava. A equally popular four wheel-drive track passes Mt. Laufafell (a hyaloclastite table-mountain, stapi). Some 10 large and small scoria craters highlight the surrounding area, along with a row of impressive explosive vents (a maar row) called Skyggnisvötn. If some of the eruptive units at Laufafell are contemporaneous with the Laugahraun lava and the Veiðivötn eruption around AD871, the eruptive fissure must have reached a total length of 60-70 kilometres.

■ An invasion from the north

Though the volcanic activity is rather sluggish (only 1.0 km^3 in 10,000 years), the volcanic history is very interesting. It is evident that the latest acid and partly obsidian-like lavas in the Torfajökull Volcanic System erupted at the same time as basaltic lavas from fissures in the nearby Veiðivötn region which belongs to the rift zone. In both cases white tephra from Torfajökull and black tephra from Veiðivötn form double coloured layers, one of which is the "Settlementlayer" (around AD 871).

It appears as if fissures in the adjoining Bárðarbunga Volcanic System opened up into the Torfajökull Volcanic System during rifting episodes. Two alternatives follow: injections of basaltic magma from the other system into the Torfajökull magma chamber (at a 10-km depth) may trigger eruptions from the chamber, or rifts without any injections may facilitate acid magma to ascend from the chamber (see p. 96). Both processes could be caused by the rift zone propagating southwards into the 2-million-year-old South Iceland Volcanic Zone (Eastern Volcanic Zone) to which the Torfajökull Volcanic System belongs.

This propagation is further indicated by the changes taken place within the South Iceland Seismic Zone. As this east-west trending fracture zone (ocean-ridge discontinuity, Fig. 95) has been moving southwards, its stress field adjusts to the push of the propagating rift to the East of the SIZS.

Boiling Mud-Pots and Ice

If one wants to experience the close contact and struggle between ice and fire, Kverkfjöll is the place to visit. With its glaciers and two calderas, Kverkfjöll rises from the northern margin of the Vatnajökull ice cap. Amidst the glaciers there is a valley of thousand smokes, boiling mud pots and blue ponds bordered by ice. The volcanic history of the Kverkfjöll Volcanic System is still far from well known.

■ A bastion of ice

The eerie lava and sand deserts north of Vatnajökull are remote and almost devoid of life. Small patches of vegetation and an occasional bird are the only signs of the living. To the south vast and white, gentle domes of the ice cap's high regions block the view, but closer to the viewer, the broad and dirty lobes of the Dyngjujökull and Brúarjökull outlet glaciers seem huge. Far to the east rises Snæfell (1,833 m), and from the middle of the margin of Vatnajökull, a big mountain massif dominates the skyline. It is called Kverkfjöll (1,920 m), cut deep by a steep, tumbling glacier (Kverkjökull). The moving ice has formed a 500 m-

63. The glaciated Kverkfjöll volcanic centre in northern Vatnajökull. The northern part of the volcanic system is clearly visible as a system of parallel tuff ridges (Kverkfjallarani). The broad lobe of the Dyngjujökull outlet glacier to the right. (Photo: Oddur Sigurðsson)

64. Kverkfjöll: an ice cave in the Kverkjökull glacier, partly formed by geothermal water. (Photo: Sigurður H. Stefnisson)

deep cleft in the mountain slopes. A system of low tuff and pillow-lava ridges and narrow valleys stretches northwards from the massif. It is named Kverkfjallarani (Fig. 63). The Kverkfjallarani region is lined by at least four Holocene volcanic fissures.

■ Two subglacial calderas

The subglacially formed ridges and recent volcanic fissures form the northern section of a volcanic system, the Kverkfjöll Volcanic System. Kverkfjöll stand out as its centre. The southern section of the fissure swarm is hidden beneath the ice masses of Vatnajökull. So also are two calderas. One of them is located in the middle of the Kverkfjöll massif (8 x 5 km) and the second one, of a similar size, is southwest of the main massif (Fig. 66). The latter is cut by sizeable faults, partly forming an ice-free, colourful valley (Hveradalur) with steam vents and mud-pots at a 1,400-1,600-m altitude, on the western edge of the massif (Fig. 65). The total length of the fissure swarm of Kverkfjöll is unknown.

The Hveradalur geothermal area (Fig. 66) and the geothermal activity elsewhere in Kverkfjöll maintain a thermal output of at least 1,300 MW. The steam and hot condensation water melt deep tunnels and caves in the adjoining glacier. A warm river flows from the snout of the Kverkfjöll glacier, creating fantastic ice tunnels (Fig. 64).

■ Rifting episodes and eruptions

The eruptive fissures in the Kverkfjallarani ridge, with the associated tholeiitic basalt lavas, and indications of unrest in the volcanic centre itself, suggest that there has been considerable eruptive activity in the Kverkfjöll Volcanic System. No sound written records exist, however, of eruptions in Kverkfjöll in early historical times. Some of the early glacial bursts in Jökulsá á Fjöllum may have been caused by subglacial eruptions in Kverkfjöll. Other unclear references of eruption clouds, seen from afar, may refer to Kverkfjöll. There are, however, at least three reliable references to small volcanic eruptions in Kverkfjöll in the 20th century (1929, about 1940, and 1959). A 600 m-wide cauldron was blasted in the ice near Hveradalur during the latest event, rimmed by dark ejecta.

At Kverkfjallarani, the evidence of volcanic activity is much more decisive. Up to 8 km-long crater rows and fairly young lava flows (altogether covering 80 km^2) show that volcanic eruptions occurred recently in the system. Farther to the east, the Lindahraun lava may be younger than 2,800 years.

The most impressive recent volcanic fissure in the Kverkfjallarani region is a rather young one. It is termed the Biskupsfell Fissure. This row of explosion craters and scoria and spatter cones, partly forming a "fire chasm", is located centrally in the Kverkfjallarani ridge. The eruption may have been associated with a rifting episode and was short but forceful. High discharge rates of fluid magma and intense lava fountains led to lots of welded scoria and lava lumps which cover nearby ridges with a unique reddish blanket. The high topography resulted in rare and bizarre flow-structures in the cover.

65. Geothermal fields high up in the Kverkfjöll volcanic centre: in Hveradalur valley, the coexistence of steam vents, mud pots and glacier is quite intriguing.
(Photo: Ari Trausti Guðmundsson)

66. *The two calderas of the Kverkfjöll Volcanic System. The fault borders the Hveradalur valley. The cauldron was formed in 1959, possibly due to volcanic or geothermal activity.*

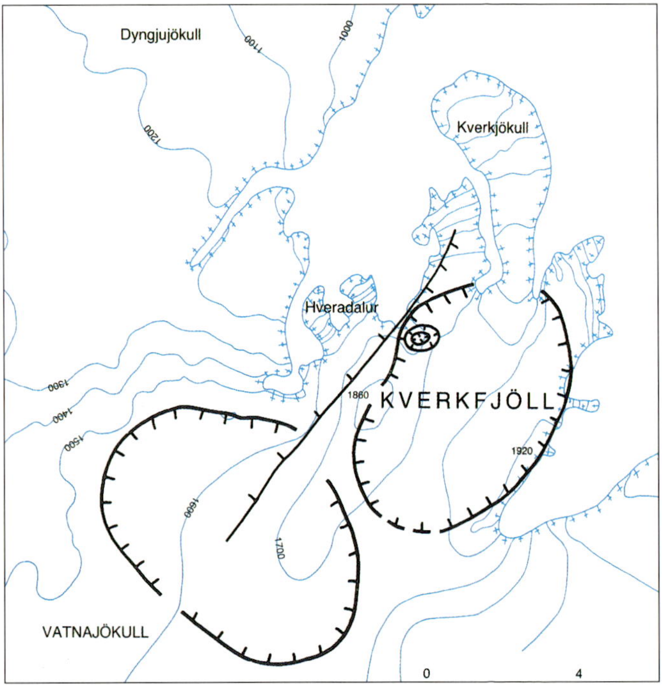

The tephra and lava of the Biskupsfell Fires amount to nearly 0.38 km³.

■ The presence of the hot spot

The volcanoes of the western and northern parts of Vatnajökull are located almost directly above the central regions of the Icelandic hot spot (top of mantle plume). This may ensure vigorous volcanic activity in this region for a long time on the human scale. At least 80 eruptions seem to have occurred in Vatnajökull in historical times only. The presence of the hot spot is indicated by data from seismic research and also by certain variations of the chemical content of eruptives along a line across Iceland. Measurements of the electrical resistivity at deep levels in the crust and adjoining mantle (magnetotelluric measurements) as well as gravity surveys show a partially molten layer beneath Iceland, rooted below the central regions (Chapter 20).

The northwestward migration of the whole plate system has gradually made the stationary mantle plume (hot spot) approach the Vatnajökull area. The main effect so far is evident: rift zone fissures within and west of Vatnajökull rift propagate southwards into the South Iceland Volcanic Zone. A side effect may be manifested in boosted volcanic activity in the easternmost central volcanoes like Kverkfjöll and Öræfajökull. They could end up as centres at the western border of a new rift zone which "jumps" eastwards in due time.

Recent research in the Torfajökull Volcanic System has led to discussions on the location of the hot spot. The data from Torfajökull may be interpreted as if the hot spot is now located beneath the South Iceland Volcanic Zone.

Iceland's Largest Mountain

The enormous bulk of the old and glaciated Öræfajökull central volcano towers above lower regions of the Skaftafell National Park. Its highest peak, Hvannadalshnúkur, is Iceland's highest summit, 2,119 m. Two registered eruptions, the former a fierce one in 1362, have occurred in Öræfajökull and destroyed both fertile land and farms.

■ Ice-clad with a hot core

The broad, white shoulders of Öræfajökull (2,119 m) are a prominent landmark of Southern Iceland. Seen from the east or west, this enormous mountain looks more like a cluster of peaks than a stratovolcano (Fig. 67). Some 13 peaks higher than 1,500 m tower from a summit plateau and the high flanks. But viewed from the south, the nature of Öræfajökull is evident: the steep and heavily glaciated cone is indeed a very old and classic central volcano. The volume is 100-200 km^3, similar to 2 or 3 of the other Icelandic stratovolcanoes.

A cauldron, about 4 km in diameter, is hidden beneath the ice on Öræfajökull's summit. It is 500-600 m deep, and steep glaciers flow over the rim down to the base of the mountain, with white peaks rising between them.

■ Two destructive eruptions

The more or less tholeiitic rocks of Öræfajökull were erupted onto old Tertiary bedrock. The bulk of the eruptives are acid, intermediate or basaltic

67. The huge bulk of the Öræfajökull stratovolcano (2,119 m). A deep summit cauldron is filled with glacier ice which branches into many steep glaciers. The volcano erupted in 1362 and 1727. (Photo: Ragnar Th. Sigurðsson)

rocks, younger than 700,000 years. Öræfajökull's volcanic history is unknown except for the eruptions of 1362 and 1727 and a possible catastrophic eruption on its southern flanks a very long time ago.

The event in 1362 was an extremely powerful plinian eruption, one of the largest of its kind in Iceland for thousands of years, and ranks among the more forceful on a world scale. It poured 5-10 km^3 of white acid pumice over Southeast and East Iceland as well as the sea off the south coast. Devastating glacier bursts turned much of the fertile land around the volcano into a desert and 30-50 South Iceland farms are said to have been temporarily abandoned or destroyed because of the floods and the pumice. Some people perished and domestic animals suffered.

The latter historical event occurred in the summer of 1727. The eruption was much smaller than the earlier one. Only 0.25 km^3 of basaltic pumice were emitted and possibly some lava. The glacier bursts were extremely powerful and carried quantities of water, boulders, sand and glacial ice to the small community of the Öræfi district (Fig. 68). It took the ice decades to melt. Three people perished, as did domestic animals, and a few houses were swept away.

The vicar Jón Þorláksson of Sandfell, at the foot of Mt. Öræfajökull, describes the beginning of the eruption in 1727 as follows:

"... people not only felt many and horrible tremors but also heard high

68. Large glacier bursts (jökulhlaups) accompanied the Öræfajökull eruptions in historical times. Sand, gravel and boulders from the 1727 burst are spread over large areas as seen here, south of the abandoned Sandfell farm and church site. (Photo: Halldór Kjartansson)

69. The proud Mt. Snæfell (1,833 m). This extinct or dormant volacno is one of Iceland's highest mountains. It supports small summit and flank glaciers.
(Photo: Ari Trausti Guðmundsson)

cracks which resembled thunders. All loose objects in our houses were thrown around and it seemed that the buildings would collapse as would the mountains behind us. However, all the houses withstood the shakings but our fears were still deepened by the fact that none of us would know what peril awaited us or where it would come from. At 9 in the morning three deep thunders were heard, louder than the other cracks, followed by water floods or eruptions of which the last was the largest, sweeping swiftly away horses and other domestic animals in their way. The glacier ice followed slowly downwards to the lowlands like molten metal poured from a smelter ... the glacier broke up and some of the icebergs entered the sea but others stranded at the foot of the mountain. Now, the air became filled with fire and ash and relentless thunders; the mist and rain of ash was so thick that we could not distinguish night from day due to the darkness caused by the black dust; the only light we saw was the glow from the earthly fire that had broken its wat into 5 or 6 crevices in the mountain ..."

■ A dying volcano?

Öræfajökull is a fairly new volcano and it rises from a much older bedrock. Its location is something of an enigma. Öræfajökull is located well outside the active volcanic zone: the South Iceland Volcanic Zone. Scientists have suggested that it may owe its existence to a fault, linking it to the main rift zone northwest of Öræfajökull, or it may belong to an additional volcanic (flank) zone adjacent to the rift zone and the SIVZ. That zone could lie, subglacially to a large extent, from Öræfajökull via Esjufjöll to a still younger but probably extinct (or dormant) central volcano Snæfell (1,833 m), northeast of Vatnajökull. Snæfell has grown rapidly but shows no imminent signs of postglacial activity (Fig. 69). The Öræfajökull-Snæfell flank zone could be explained as the first signs of a rift zone which is developing east of the present one due to the apparent eastward migration of the hot spot.

Whatever the explanation, Öræfajökull is, on a human scale, a rather sluggish but certainly by no means timid volcano.

Iceland's Worst Natural Catastrophe

A 25 km-long fire fissure and 130 craters are an impressive feature indeed. The Laki Fissure emitted one of the largest lava flows in recent history only a little over 200 years ago: 14,000,000,000 m^3. In addition, quantities of tephra, volcanic gases and acid droplets filled the air. This caused a terrible famine in Iceland and temporarily influenced the climate of the northern hemisphere.

■ 130 craters

About 35 km north of the small, pleasant village of Kirkjubæjarklaustur, a small tuff mountain called Laki stands out of a lava field. Standing atop of it, a 13 km-long row of scoria and spatter cones is visible, lined up to the southwest. An equally long volcanic fissure runs to the northeast (Fig. 71). The total number of volcanic vents on both sections of the fissure is 130 but the fissure itself comprises 10 en echelon segments (shifted in a sub-parallel fashion) representing successive events. The segments are 2-5 km long. Most events started with a short phreato-magmatic phase, followed by an explosive (strombolian) phase to be concluded shortly by the longest effusive, lava-producing phase.

Old and large crater rows may be seen south and north of this stupendous volcanic fissure which is called the Laki Fissure. It dates from 1783 and is the site of one of the most productive lava eruptions on Earth in recorded times, and is also to be blamed for the worst natural catastrophe to hit Iceland in historical times. The episode is called Skaftáreldar (Skaftá Fires) in Icelandic, followed by Móðuharðindi (Haze Famine). In English literature the series of eruptions is termed the Laki Eruption.

■ 8,000 m^3 of lava per second

In late May and early June 1783, people in Southern Iceland felt many earthquakes. The unrest may have stirred up some fear because the 18th century, up to that time, had been very disturbing regarding volcanic activity in Iceland. Katla and Hekla had both erupted violently, Öræfajökull had blown its lid, the Mývatn Fires had continued for years and numerous eruptions occurred in Vatnajökull.

On June 8th a large section of the southwestern part of the Laki fissure opened up. The eruption was probably associated with a rifting episode prior to the eruption and manifested by the earthquakes, and rifting events continued during the following months. A terrible cloud of pumice, ash and magmatic vapour enveloped the farming districts south of the eruption site. Soon a broad stream of lava flowed into the lowlands. The lava discharge was 7,200-8,700 m^3 per second.

■ Up to 1,400 m high lava-fountains

By July 20th some farms were already engulfed by lava or abandoned, but the lava front finally ground to a halt a few kilometres west of Kirkjubæjarklaustur. It had already covered a distance of more than 40 km. On the 29th, the

70. Eldhraun (Skaftáreldahraun), the huge lava flow from the Lakagígar craters (1783). It is a typical scoria lava (aa), with ropy lava patches (pahoehoe) but covered by thick mosses in the lower regions. (Photo: Halldór Kjartansson)

eruption continued from a new north-eastern section, immediately after the activity ceased in the other section. The lava fountains on the fissure, up to 800-1,400 m high, formed an impressive wall of magma and a vast amount of tephra was released from its top. Now the lava flowed to the south somewhat east of Kirkjubæjarklaustur, and still more farms were destroyed.

This eruption went on until early February 1784. In the autumn of 1783 a tephra eruption was seen in the western part of Vatnajökull (southwest of or in Grímsvötn?), and in 1784 more volcanic activity in the ice cap, in Grímsvötn, was noticed. It continued until May 1785. Glacier bursts occurred in the rivers Súla, Núpsvötn and Skeiðará.

■ Millions of tons of lava, tephra and gases

The Laki eruption was a grand-scale episode. The eruptive volume is 14-15 km^3, of which tephra is 0.75 km^3 or 750 million m^3 (400 million m^3 as dense rock). The lava covers 580-600 km^2, enough to cover one-tenth of Iceland with a 1 m-thick blanket (Fig. 72). Some 400-500 million tons of gases emerged from the interior of the Earth and of the 140 million tons of sulphur dioxide a large part formed at least 80 million tons of sulphuric acid. Some of the acid fell as rain over

Southern Iceland but the rest remained as very small droplets (aerosol), floating high up in the air along with minute, glassy tephra grains. This "haze" was carried by winds to Europe and W-Asia.

The lava is a remarkably homogeneous basalt (tholeiite), less developed than eruptives from Grímsvötn, suggesting a direct source in the crust-mantle boundary (from a magma reservoir) rather than a lateral magma injection from a shallow magma chamber (beneath Grímsvötn). The subglacial eruptions in Vatnajökull during and after the Laki event were probably also induced by magma from the same reservoir meeting, and partly ponding in, the Grímsvötn magma chamber. A rifting episode may have triggered the scenario. These issues are under debate. So are also the suggestions that the present Laki craters could in fact be remnants of three volcano-tectonic episodes, two of which are much older than the Skaftáreldar Fires (Laki eruption in AD1783).

■ The Haze Famine

The Laki lava destroyed or damaged 20 farms and a large area of fertile land was temporarily of no use to farmers due to the tephra cover and poisoned vegetation. The lava-covered land was, of course, lost. Today, mosses, grass, lymegrass and willows thrive in the lava (Fig. 70).

No lives were lost during the eruption, but events were to take a different course in the years 1784 and 1785. The blue and poisonous vapour released by the cooling eruptives was carried by winds far over Iceland. Crops were meagre and poisoned in some areas and both people and animals became sick and weak from breathing unhealthy air, consuming polluted water and eating too little or poisoned food. In addition, pack-ice drifted to Iceland. The haze and the cloud of acid droplets or fine-grained ash also reduced the amount of solar radiation, in Iceland and on a worldscale. The cooling of the climate added still more "bad years" in Iceland to the already severe seasons of 1782 and 1783. The effects of these events were catastrophic. About 20% of the population and more than 50% of domestic animals perished. There were serious discussions in Denmark of moving the Icelanders to Jutland, but no action was taken.

A volcanic fissure eruption of similar magnitude as the Laki eruption is possible at any time within the main rift zone of Iceland. It would pose great problems to the Icelanders and could for example affect air traffic in the North Atlantic region and the weather on a large scale.

71. A part of the 25 km-long Lakagígar (Eldborgir) crater row from 1783-1784. Scoria and spatter cones predominate. (Photo: Ágúst Guðmundsson)

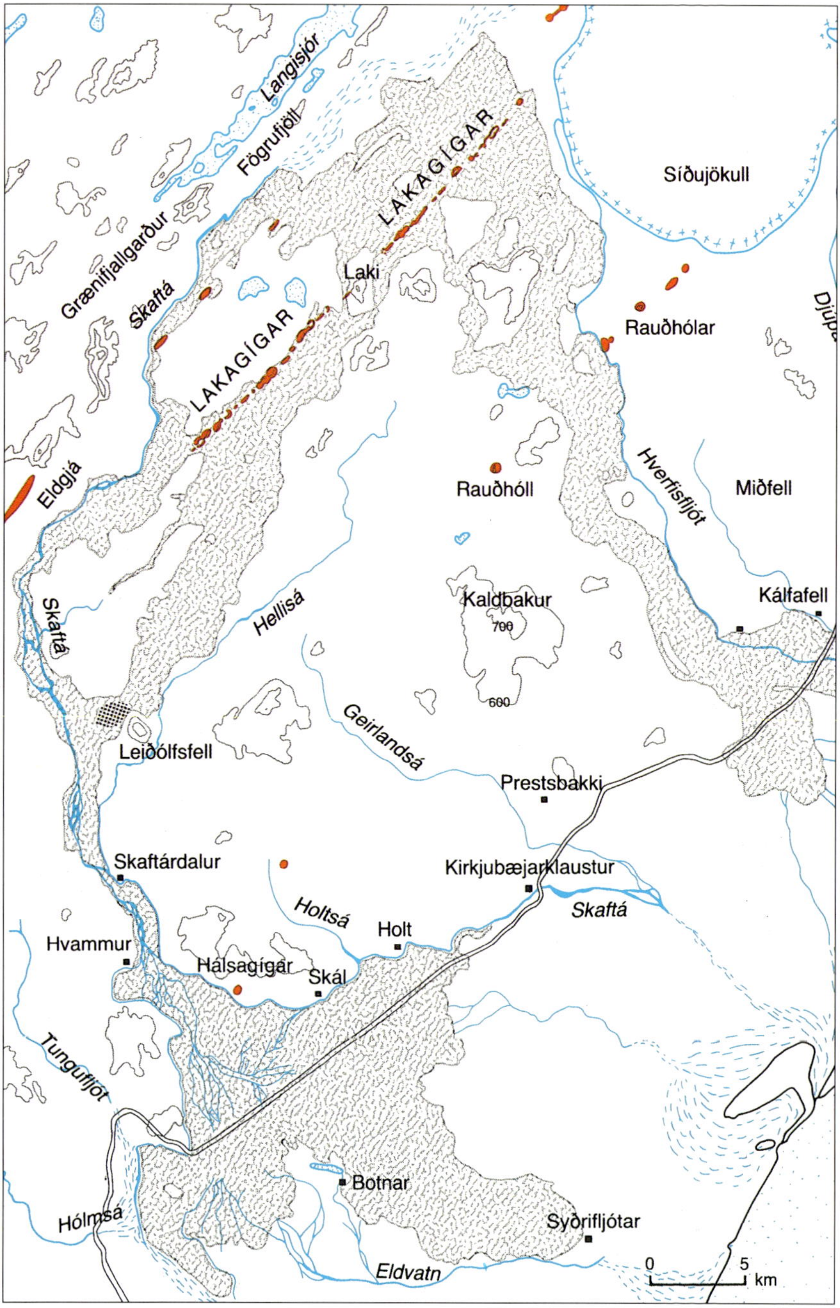

72. A recent map of the Skaftáreldarhraun lava (Lakagígar crater row, 1783-1784) and the associated volcanic fissure.

The Long Rifts

The Bárðarbunga Volcanic System is one of the lesser known but large volcanic systems in Iceland. Its centre is buried under hundreds of metres of glacier ice but the long fissure swarm extends dozens of kilometres on ice-free land. There, long rows of imposing craters, volcanogenic lakes and faults can be traced to the southwest while volcanic fissures cut into a moon-like area in the north.

■ A long volcanic system

When flying over the central highlands and the interior of Iceland, we notice seemingly endless tuff-ridges, chains of small lakes (Veiðivötn), fissures and crater rows west of the huge Vatnajökull ice cap. These structures disappear underneath the western margin of the ice cap where high glaciated domes stand out, notably the 2,000 m-high Bárðarbunga (Fig. 73). Farther to the north, fissures and crater rows reappear on the ridge of Dyngjuháls and are lined towards Iceland's largest lava

73. Bárðarbunga, Vatnajökull ice cap. Glaciers tumble down from a high ice dome which conceals a large central volcano with a 600 m-deep caldera. The large dark spot in the background is the Grímsvötn caldera. The two smaller spots to the right of Grímsvötn are the Skaftá cauldrons formed by geothermal heat melting glacier ice above a high-temperature area. (Photo: Oddur Sigurðsson)

74. The Vatnaöldur fissure. This long fissure is set with some lava-producing craters but also with a magnificent row of large tephra rings and maars, dating from approximately AD871. (Photo: Ingibjörg Kaldal)

shield, Trölladyngja (1,510 m, Fig. 28). Because of the ice cover in the central parts of this volcanic region, it is not known whether all the volcanic structures and fissures form one fissure swarm or not. If so, it would be the longest in the rift zone. It measures up to 160 km in length, but only 10-20 km in width.

■ Two ice clad calderas

Recent radio echo soundings show that an 11 km-wide and 600 to 700 m-deep caldera exists below the firn and ice of Bárðarbunga. This large volcanic centre has no recorded volcanic history, but it is the location of many, often strong, earthquakes.

South of Bárðarbunga another dome-shaped structure rises from the flat outlet glaciers: at Hamarinn (1,573 m), another central volcano with a caldera rests under ice cover. It has an equally obscure volcanic history as Bárðarbunga.

There is still no conclusive evidence of a connection between the northern and southern parts of the long fissure swarm. They might be two independent systems, meeting beneath the Vatnajökull ice cap. The existence of the two volcanic centres, Bárðarbunga and Hamarinn, at the junction, and the identical chemical characteristics of eruptives from both parts, suggest, however, that the fissure swarm and the two centres form one system, the Bárðarbunga Volcanic System.

■ The Veiðivötn-Jökulheimar region: lakes, tephra rings and rifts

The parallel hyaloclastite or tuff-ridges, separated by shallow, broad valleys and long lakes or river beds north of the Torfajökull area, all look rather alike. They are remains of subglacial eruptions in the southern part of the Bárðarbunga Volcanic System. The Holocene structures are of a much more varied breed: rows of tephra rings, scoria crater rows, crater lakes (maars), rifts and faults (Fig. 75). The largest faults form a long and spectacular rift valley (graben) called Heljargjá.

Volcanic activity in the Veiðivötn-Jökulheimar region has been vigorous for the past 7,000-8,000 years, producing 75 eruptive units.

About 7,800 BP an enormous lava flow gushed from a now covered fissure in the western part of the region. It had the astounding volume of 21 km^3, an area of over 900 km^2, and reached the sea 120 km southwest of its source! The "ring road" crosses this Þjórsárhraun lava east of the town of Selfoss (Fig. 79). The lava is made of tholeiite and is the largest of its kind in the world within postglacial time (Holocene).

During the following 6,000 years, at least 8 more lava flows emerged from the area near Heljargjá, ranging in area from 55 to 275 km^2 (up to 3.9 km^3): the so-called Tungnaárhraun lavas.

■ The fierce historical eruptions

The historical eruptions in the southern part of the Bárðarbunga Volcanic System seem to be confined to the eastern rim and central region of the fissure swarm. Three distinct volcano-tectonic episodes have been defined: the Vatnaöldur Eruptions in about AD871, the Veiðivötn Fires in 1480, and finally the Tröllahraun Eruptions not far from Hamarinn in 1862-1864. Prior to these episodes, eruptions occurred in the Veiðivötn region and in the Torfajökull Volcanic System (AD150) and a still older episode dates from about 1200BC.

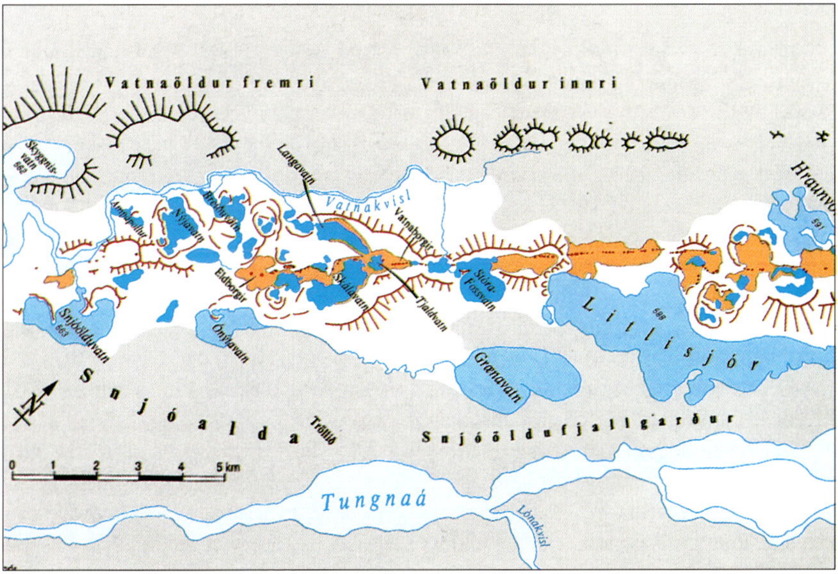

75. The Veiðivötn area. This lake basin was the scene of a series of intense volcanic eruptions in AD1480. The long row of craters includes large tephra rings, maars and spatter or scoria cones, but the fissure continues eastwards, totalling some 60 km.

76. The Fossavötn lakes in the Veiðivötn group. Craters, depressions and lava dams created this fascinating area in AD1480. (Photo: Ágúst Guðmundsson)

During the first two episodes, the events also triggered eruptions in the Torfajökull Volcanic System (Chapter 14).

The first of the three volcano-tectonic episodes, in around AD871, included an explosive (phreatic) eruption on a 60 km-long discontinuous fissure. It spread tephra over large parts of Iceland (3.3 km^3). A part of this tephra has been used as a lead-layer in dating where traceable tephra deposits are utilized as age markers (tephrochronology). The layer is the so-called "Settlement-layer". The most spectacular part of the volcanic fissure is the tephra rings and tephra cones of Vatnaöldur (Fig. 75). The Hrafntinnuhraun lava (acid rock) in the Torfajökull Volcanic System dates from the same episode.

The second episode, the Veiðivötn eruptions, ca. 1480, gave birth to a mixed 40 km-long row of beautiful tephra craters, most of which contain emerald green and blue lakes, and many scoria and spatter cones. These are associated with lavas (0.4 km^3 in total). The largest part of the eruptives consists of 3.5 km^3 of airborne tephra. The lakes are called Veiðivötn and Hraunvötn and substitute partly for the older Fiskivötn in the basin where the volcanic activity was most intense (Fig. 75 and 76).

The third episode included 5-10 events, all consisting of short-lived fissure lava eruptions in the remote Jökulheimar region, close to the western margin of Vatnajökull. The volcano-tectonic episode lasted for 27 months. The fissure is 16 km long (10 off-set segments) and is set with 50-60 small craters. The lava covers 28 km², including parts of the Heljargjá graben, and has a volume of 0.3 km³ (Fig. 78). The eruptions were not observed at close range and the craters and lava flow were first described in 1927.

The high ratio of tephra in the Vatnaöldur and Veiðivötn eruptions is attributed to a high level of groundwater in the area. When the magma ascended through thick lenses of groundwater, large amounts of the molten rock were granulated by rapid cooling and large quantities of tephra blown off into the air during the first events of the episode. After a while the fissure segments produced lava.

■ The Dyngjuháls region: a moon-like area

The barren landscape northeast of Vatnajökull is lined with crater rows and rough, dark lava flows. On the Dyngjuháls ridge there are at least 8 relatively young volcanic fissures and associated lavas (Fig. 77). They probably belong to the northern part of the Bárðarbunga Volcanic System or might be, as outlined above, part of an independent fissure swarm.

The Dyngjuháls fissures terminate near the Askja volcano (Dyngjufjöll) in the north and they disappear into the broad lobe of the Dyngjujökull outlet glacier in the southwest.

Tephra layers and written sources indicate that there was volcanic activity at Dyngjuháls and in Dyngjujökull throughout historical time. The most notable episodes are a large eruption in 1477 (more or less coinciding with the Veiðivötn Fires) and a series of eruptions between 1680 and 1730.

The subglacial eruptions were followed by glacier bursts along the river Jökulsá á Fjöllum. From 1797 into the early 20th century some unconfirmed reports of "eruptions at the northern margins of Vatnajökull" may refer to eruptions in this remote area.

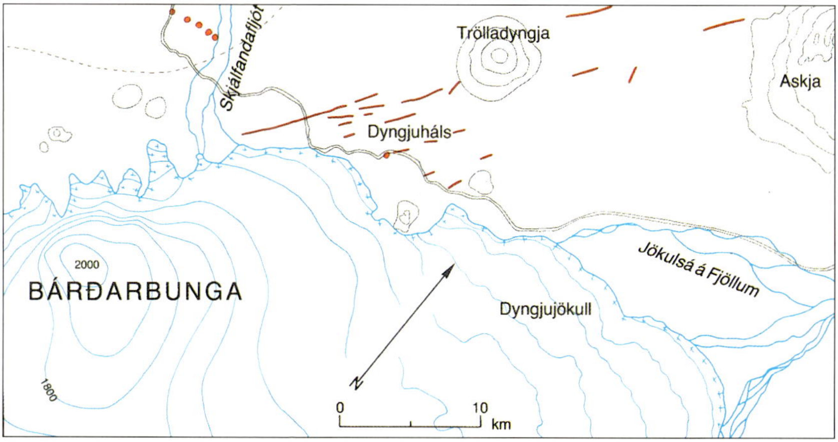

77. Volcanic fissures at the Dyngjuháls ridge. Note the Bárðarbunga volcanic centre and the Trölladyngja lava shield. The small crater row west of Dyngjuháls belongs to the Tungnafellsjökull Volcanic System.

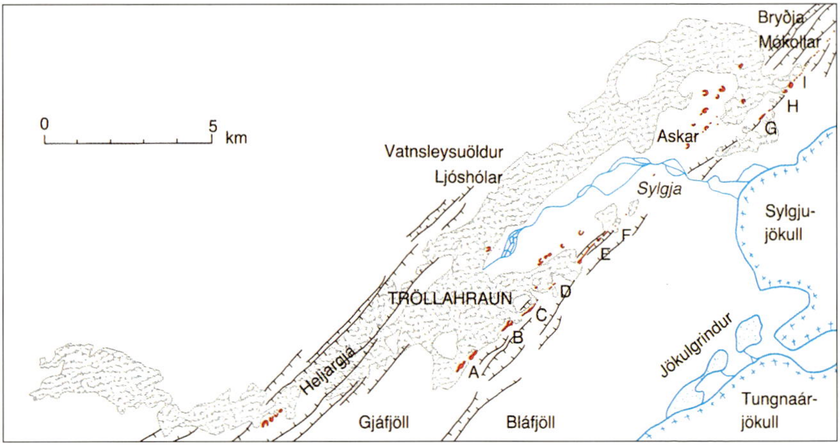

78. The northeastern part of the Heljargjá graben and the Tröllahraun lava flow from 1862-1864. Some 10 off-set (en echelon) volcanic fissure segments represent individual events during this volcano-tectonic episode (A-I). Askar and Bryðja are much older craters.

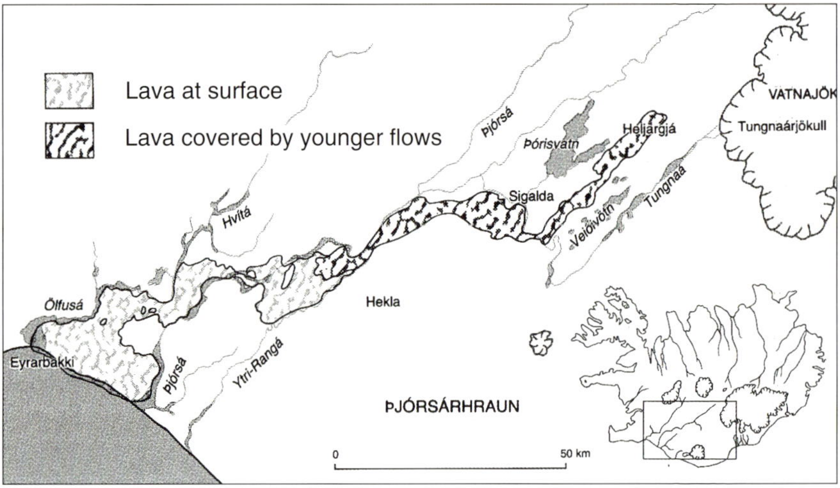

79. Possibly the biggest postglacial (Holocene) lava flow on Earth: the Þjórsárhraun lava, 7,800 years old. Estimated volume is 21 km³ and the area 930 km².

A Crowned Chain

The beautiful white cone of the Snæfellsjökull volcano crowns a chain of mountains which form the backbone of the long Snæfellsnes peninsula in Western Iceland. It is regarded as an active but dormant centre of one out of three volcanic systems on the peninsula. Only one eruption has occurred in historical times on Snæfellsnes; the eruption of Rauðhálsar in about AD900, mentioned in the medieval "Book of Settlement" (Landnámabók).

■ Jules Verne's volcano

In Western Iceland a very large bay, Faxaflói, is cradled by the boot-shaped Reykjanes Peninsula in the south and the narrow but high Snæfellsnes (Snæfells Peninsula) in the north. The latter is characterized by a chain of steep-sided mountains (up to 1,000-1,400 m). Many geological structures in this region originated in recent volcanic eruptions: red scoria craters, steep lava fields and banks of whitish pumice. Others are undoubtedly older, such as coarse-grained intrusions and thick sequences of lava flows.

The peninsula is only 10-30 km wide but 80 km long, and the skyline bristles with varied peaks around the 700-

80. The Snæfellsjökull stratovolcano (1,446 m). The mountain is a volcanic centre of an elongated volcanic system (trending northwest-southeast). The last eruption occurred some 1,800 years ago. (Photo by Ari Trausti Guðmundsson)

1,000 m altitude mark. One mountain, however, a fairly young geological structure, rises high above the surrounding highlands. It is the majestic stratovolcano Snæfellsjökull. This ice-capped mountain (1,446 m) can be seen from over 100 km away (Fig. 80). It was once thought to be the highest mountain in Iceland and earned fame from Jules Verne's "A Voyage to the Centre of the Earth", where he portrayed the crater as the starting point for an incredible venture (1864).

Three volcanic systems occur on the peninsula. They have a sub-parallel (en echelon) arrangement, but in a northwesterly direction instead of the more normal northeasterly direction found in the central parts of Iceland. The region differs also in other aspects from the main rift zone. It is a non-rifting flank zone, producing rocks from the alkalic series.

■ Old roots

The Snæfellsnes volcanic zone has, in fact, quite old roots. The bulk of the bedrock of the central parts of the peninsula is as much as 7-9 million years old. There are at least two old and eroded central volcanoes in this area. All these older volcanic rocks date from the era when the main rift zone bisected Iceland in the Snæfellsnes region. The rift zone then "jumped" to the east, 6-7 million years ago, due to the northwesterly drift of the Icelandic block over the mantle plume (see Chapter 20).

After a long period of inactivity,

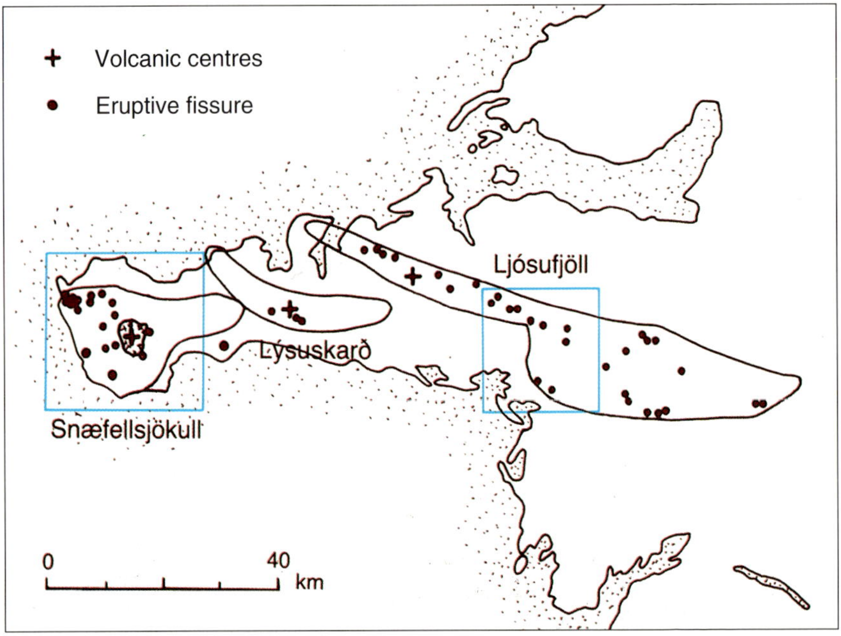

81. The three volcanic systems on the Snæfellsnes peninsula (from left to right): Snæfellsjökull Volcanic System, Lýsuskarð Volcanic System and Ljósufjöll Volcanic System.

82. A glaciated stratovolcano: Snæfellsjökull (1,446 m). It is regarded as an active volcanic centre of a volcanic system but has not erupted for 1,700-1,800 years. One of the Hólahólar scoria and spatter craters in the volcanic system is seen in the foreground.
(Photo: Halldór Kjartansson)

volcanism was renewed some 2 million years ago. New fault lines and stress regimes may have revived the volcanic activity. It commenced in the central part of the peninsula and then spread to the west and east. The associated volcanoes and tectonic lineaments group into three distinct and active fissure swarms (Fig. 81), forming volcanic systems, each with a centre characterized by a topographic high and by acid rocks. A fourth system, farther inland, is now extinct, but the others have been active recently.

■ Three volcanic systems

The westernmost volcanic system on the Snæfellsnes peninsula is the Snæfellsjökull Volcanic System. It consists of at least 10 postglacial crater rows or single, recent craters, in addition to the beautiful and symmetrical stratovolcano which is somewhat older than 700,000 years. The lesser volcanic vents are scoria craters, some of which are easily spotted from the road encircling Snæfellsjökull. The mountain itself contains a huge and partly collapsed central crater, filled with ice. The mountain slopes are also partly glaciated (12 km^2) or covered with thick, fluted andesite lava flows (Fig. 82). Some were emitted by visible craters on the mountain flanks. The volcanic system measures 20 by 30 km and some 20-30 eruptions can be attributed to its volcanic vents, none of which is, however, of historical age. The last two eruptions of Snæfellsjökull occurred 3,900 and 1,750 BP.

Next in line is the Lýsuskarð Volcanic System. It is located in the central highlands on the peninsula, with only 2 recent eruptive units. There are, however, magnificent cascades of solidified lava to be seen where molten rock once plunged down the southern slopes of the highlands (e.g. the Bláfeldarhraun lava). This system is the smallest one of the three: 30 km long and 5 km wide.

The largest and easternmost system is the Ljósufjöll Volcanic System, a 90 km-long and up to 20 km-broad fissure swarm with its centre in the shapely Ljósufjöll mountains. The northernmost craters are in the Berserkjahraun lava flows (about 3,800-4,000 years old) between the towns of Grundarfjörður and Stykkishólmur. The southernmost volcanic fissure is in the upper Borgarfjörður region: the Grábrók craters (less than 3,600 years old). In between these two volcanic sites are more than 20 other volcanic fissures lined with fine scoria cones which emitted scoria lava flows (aa), or with symmetrical lava rings associated with a mixture of rough aa and ropy pahoehoe lava flows, dotted with lava caves.

The basalt of the Lýsuskarð and Ljósufjöll systems and the rocks of Snæfellsjökull and its flanking craters belong to the alkalic series. The magma is thought to be derived from at least a depth of 20-25 km in contrast to the much shallower magma-generating regions beneath the rift zone.

■ Violent eruptions

The main road to Snæfellsnes passes a few of the volcanic fissures in the Ljósufjöll Volcanic System. In the valley of Hnappadalur, the reddish lava ring of Eldborg is clearly seen (at least 5,000 years old, Fig. 83). So are the two high and pyramid-shaped Rauðamelskúlur, red scoria craters (2,600 years old, Fig. 84). Nearby is the

83. The Eldborg lava ring, W. Iceland. Short effusive lava eruptions produce craters, made of firm spatter walls. This is the largest crater on a short 5,000-year-old volcanic fissure in the Ljósufjöll Volcanic System. (Photo: Páll Stefánsson)

84. Columnar basalt lava and a much younger scoria cone: Rauðamelskúla in Hnappadalur, W. Iceland. (Photo: Ágúst Guðmundsson)

only historical eruptive unit on the peninsula. A lava flow and a single, bulky scoria crater, called Rauðhálsar, dates from about AD900. The eruption and the lava flow, which supposedly destroyed a farm, are mentioned in the medieval Book of Settlements (Landnámabók).

No historical eruptions have occurred in the Snæfellsjökull Volcanic System. All the eruptive fissures in the lowlands around Snæfellsjökull are more than 1,100 years old. Some of the lava flows which are traced to craters on the slopes of the mountain might be somewhere between 1,100 and 1,800 years old, but the stratovolcano itself has erupted only twice during the past 4,000-5,000 years. The former eruption occurred around 2000BC, producing voluminous acid tephra. The latter which dates from around AD200 was a violent, explosive tephra eruption (a plinian eruption), probably followed by lava emission. The northern rim of the central crater may have collapsed during this event and 20-50 cm of grey pumice covered a large area to the north and northeast of the volcano.

The lava flows in the Snæfellsnes Volcanic System have entered the sea at many locations. Marine erosion and the encounter between sea and glowing lava have created interesting formations, for example at Arnarstapi and Hellnar. Interesting volcanic craters or structures include the Bárðarlaug maar, the Lóndrangar crater (Fig. 85 and 86) plugs and the Búðaklettur, Hólahólar and Öndverðarneshólar craters.

85. Lóndrangar crater remains. The rugged coastline around Mt. Snæfellsjökull is very interesting, due to varied and spectacular lava formations. (Photo: Ari Trausti Guðmundsson)

86. The Bárðarlaug maar. An old but postglacial (Holocene) eruptive formation, the maar was created in an explosive event. (Photo: Ari Trausti Guðmundsson)

Iceland is a Fiery Island

Plate tectonics and volcanism are key words regarding the geological history of Iceland. About 30 volcanic sytems with hundreds of volcanoes and volcanic vents are considered active at the present. A variety of magmas, almost every known type of volcano and a high rate of eruptions make Iceland an eldorado for geologists as well as geologically minded naturalists.

■ Of volcanic origin

Iceland has an area of 103,000 km^2 and rises from a large submarine platform to an altitude of 1,000 to 2,000 m. The bulk of the Icelandic block is created by volcanic activity. More than 90% of the island itself consists of numerous overlapping lava flows, commonly with a 5°-15° tilt. Interbedded are different types of sediment or tuff (5%). The lava flows are also intersected by intrusive volcanic structures such as dykes or sheets and thick flow sequences (piles) contain old magma chambers, seen as voluminous bodies of plutonic rocks or as acid outcrops. These intrusive structures and the

87. Volcanic structures in Iceland span anything from 15 million-year-old and heavily eroded cores of central volcanoes to brand-new craters and lava flows. Here, geologists are studying the fissure eruption on the Heimaey island in 1973.

(Photo: Ari Trausti Guðmundsson)

piles of lava flows are mainly exposed in the western and eastern parts of the country, where the oldest and most heavily eroded areas in Iceland are found. The closer we approach the central and younger parts of Iceland, the more fresh-looking lava flows and less eroded volcanic structures characterize the landscape (Fig. 87).

A geological explanation for similarly aged rocks successively arranged on both flanks of an active volcanic central zone is found in the theory of plate tectonics (sometimes termed continental drift or sea floor spreading). Iceland is being torn apart by tremendous forces that are manifested by plate movements on the Earth's surface. The island straddles two diverging plates, the North American plate (in the west) which moves westwards and the Eurasian plate (in the east) which moves eastwards (Fig. 88). Upwelling magma at the plate boundaries creates the Atlantic sea floor and contributes to the bedrock of Iceland.

The volcanic activity which brought Iceland about has apparently been fairly continual for the past 20-25 million years. During that time span thousands upon thousands of eruptions have added material to the complex pile of volcanic rocks. Its total thickness is about 10,000 m but the lava layers are gently sloping inwards, thus attaining a height of 1,000-1,500 m above sea level. The accumulation rate has been determined at up to thousands of metres of lava per million years, in places where magmatic pulses boosted the volcanic activity from time to time. Normally, the accumulation rate is in the order of hundreds of metres per million years. The pile resembles a heap of slightly spread stacks of cards.

Remnants of more than 50 volcanic centres (central volcanoes or silicic centres) are known in and around Iceland, each associated with numerous dykes and faults. Each such centre was active for 300,000 to 2.5 million years. The volcanic history of all these centres cannot be accounted for. But the volcanic history of the past 10,000 years (the Holocene) reveals the magnitude of Icelandic volcanism. About 30 younger volcanic centres have been active during that time, along with a few hundred volcanic fissures (Fig. 96). These eruptive fissures are now traced as rows of craters of different sizes and shapes or single craters in the landscape.

More than 250 volcanic eruptions have occurred in historical times in Iceland, i.e. the past 1,100 years since the settlement. They have occurred repeatedly in 10 out of the 30 volcanic centres and once each in hosts of volcanic fissures, producing a total of 42-48 km^3 of eruptive rocks. This means one eruption almost every five years and more than 4 km^3 of eruptives per century on average. The 20th century, however, has seen more than 30 eruptions (and 10-15 disputed or uncertain ones), thereby pushing the eruption rate to once every 3-4 years. Better surveillance and information are the main reason for the discrepancy; a sudden increase of the eruption frequency is not likely.

■ Diverging plates and hot spots

The North Atlantic Ocean began to open 65-70 million years ago (in the very early Tertiary). The continents on each side of an active spreading ridge (a long system of rift zone segments and fracture zones) moved east and west-

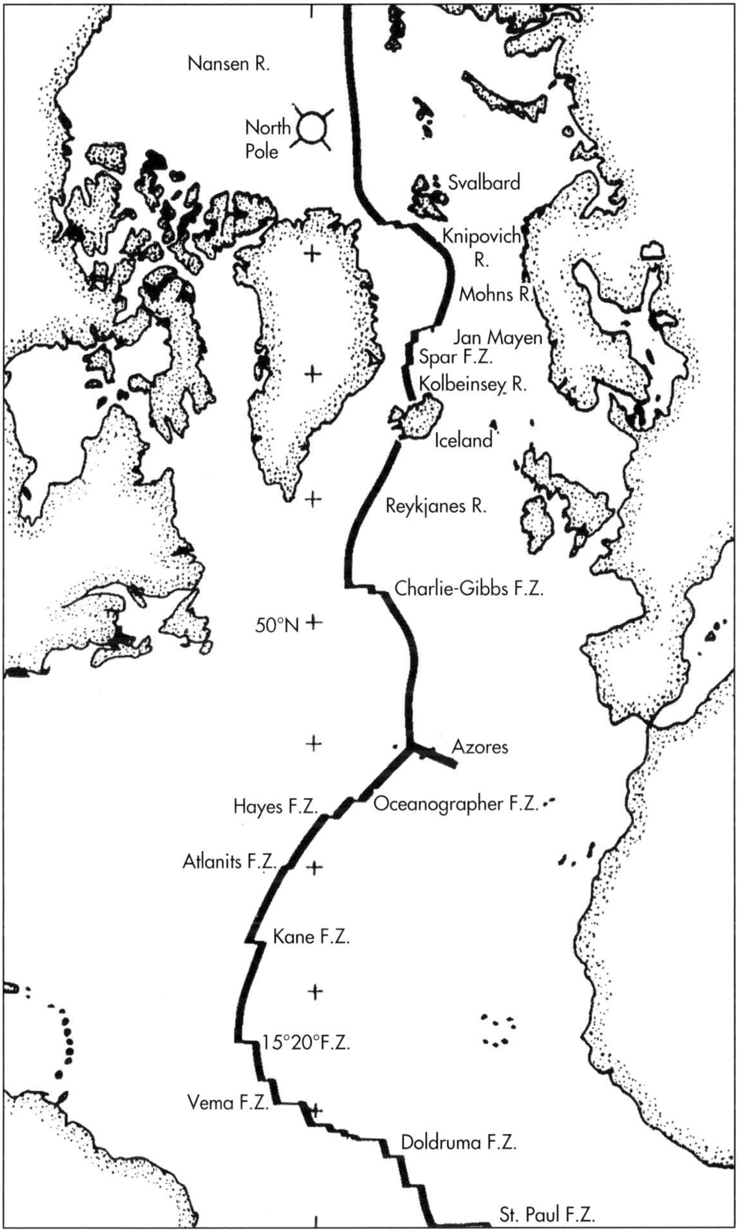

88. The divergent plate boundaries in the North Atlantic and Arctic Oceans and Iceland. Spreading ridge segments (rift zones) are offset by fracture zones (F.Z.).

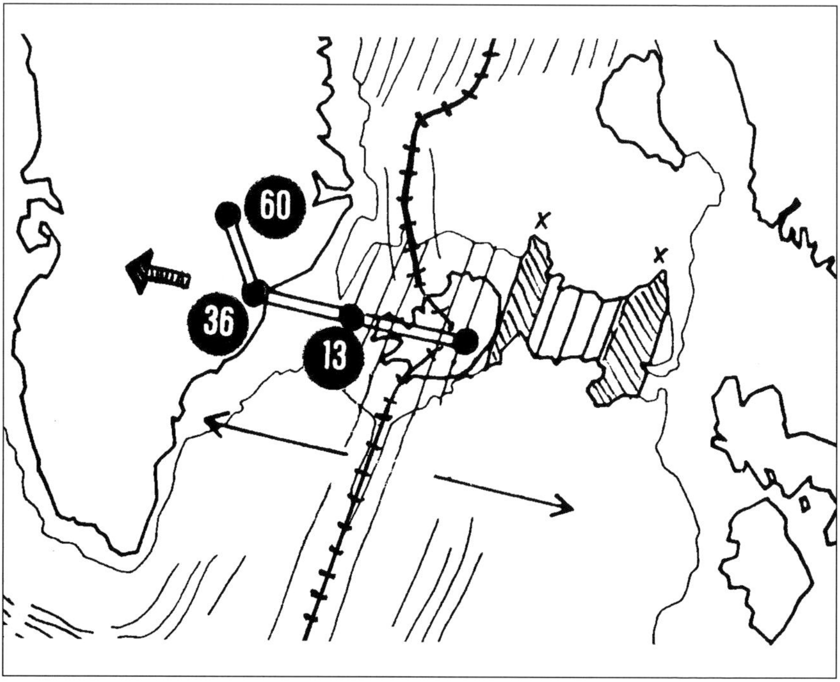

89. The hypothesis of a stationary hot spot. The diverging plates (spreading shown with thin arrows) have drifted to the northwest, relative to the mantle plume (hot spot) as shown with a thick arrow. Some 60 million years ago, the rift system was active between the areas marked by X's and the hot spot was deep inside Greenland. Some 35 million years ago the drift had placed the hot spot at the edge of Greenland. A new rift system opened up between Greenland and then non-existing Iceland. About 13-16 million years ago, the mantle plume and the rift nearly coalesced, and the combined magma production of both these sources sufficed to create the embryo of a large landmass. Vigorous volcanism, as the rift system "followed" the hot spot eastwards, resulted in the 200,000 km² Icelandic block.

wards. During the first 40 million years the spreading ridge, commonly referred to as diverging plate boundaries, was partly located east of the present Icelandic block. The ridge may have shifted from time to time but remained locally active for a long time as the Aegir Ridge (now extinct between Norway and Iceland).

The upward flow of magma below the Mid-Atlantic Ridge and the associated volcanic and intrusive activity are not sufficient to build large islands on the ridge segments, only to create new sea floor and the elevated ridge itself. The existence of Iceland points towards an additional source of magma close to the Iceland rift. And so there is: in the form of a mantle plume below the crust and a hot spot on the face of the Earth.

More than 20 hot spots have been traced on the Earth's surface. They are the surface manifestations of slow-rising and fountain-like plumes of partly molten material in the mantle. The plumes are 50-200 km in diameter.

Some are located in the vicinity of plate boundaries but others are beneath the plates. Each hot spot is characterized by an abnormally high crustal heat flux and usually by geothermal or volcanic activity. A well-known hot spot far away from plate margins brews up the volcanic activity in the Hawaiian Islands. Another hot spot is located near the Mid-Atlantic Ridge in Iceland (Fig. 89 and 95). It has slowly shifted position from Greenland to Iceland over tens of millions of years. Since the associated mantle plume is thought to be stationary, the apparent migration of the hot spot is due to the sluggish motion or drift of both plates to the northwest over the plume, more or less independent of the normal plate spreading.

In the early Tertiary, the plate spreading and the hot-spot activity resulted in extensive basaltic formations which now form parts of East Greenland, Scotland/Ireland and the Faroe Islands. Some 30-35 million years ago the northwestward drift of the plates had moved the Greenland landmass far west relative to the mantle plume so that the hot spot emerged below the eastern margin of Greenland's continental shelf. This led to the opening of a new ridge segment close to the hot spot, i.e. the spreading shifted from the old Aegir ridge to a new rift zone close to Eastern Greenland. Magma from the mantle plume could now add to the upflow of magma below the ridge segment. The northwestward drift of the plates moved the hot spot still closer to this new spreading ridge segment. Consequently, the volcanism grew more vigorous. Some 15-20 million years ago (Fig. 89), the ridge and the hot spot nearly coalesced and this led to the formation (or enlargement) of new land a few hundred kilometres off the Greenland coast: the primeval Iceland. It may have been a cluster of islands at first, a single growing island or even a bridge of land between continents.

■ Rift jumps and rifting episodes

The plates and the spreading ridge are still drifting northwestward relative to the mantle plume. The plume and the hot spot seem, therefore, to be migrating farther to the east. This has already shifted the rift segments in the Icelandic region at least once and will change the rift system further with time. Until 6-7 million years ago the rift axis stretched across the present Snæfellsnes peninsula towards the northeast. The drift of the plates had then shifted central Iceland into position above the stationary mantle plume. As a result, the rift zone shifted to the southeast, approximately to its present position. The centre of the hot spot is believed to be now somewhat southeast of central Iceland.

The northwestward drift of the plates relative to the hot spot also has created a complex zone of volcanic and seismic activity in Iceland instead of a simple straight rift through the island (Fig. 95).

The current average spreading rate in the North Atlantic measures about 2 cm per year. The spreading is not continuous but commences in local rifting episodes, lasting for days, weeks or even years with intervals of many years, decades or even centuries. The local spreading may then reach the order of some metres. Each episode is usually composed of two or more much shorter events. Many episodes separated by a long quiescent interval of time from other episodes form rifting periods. Earthquakes occur during tectonic

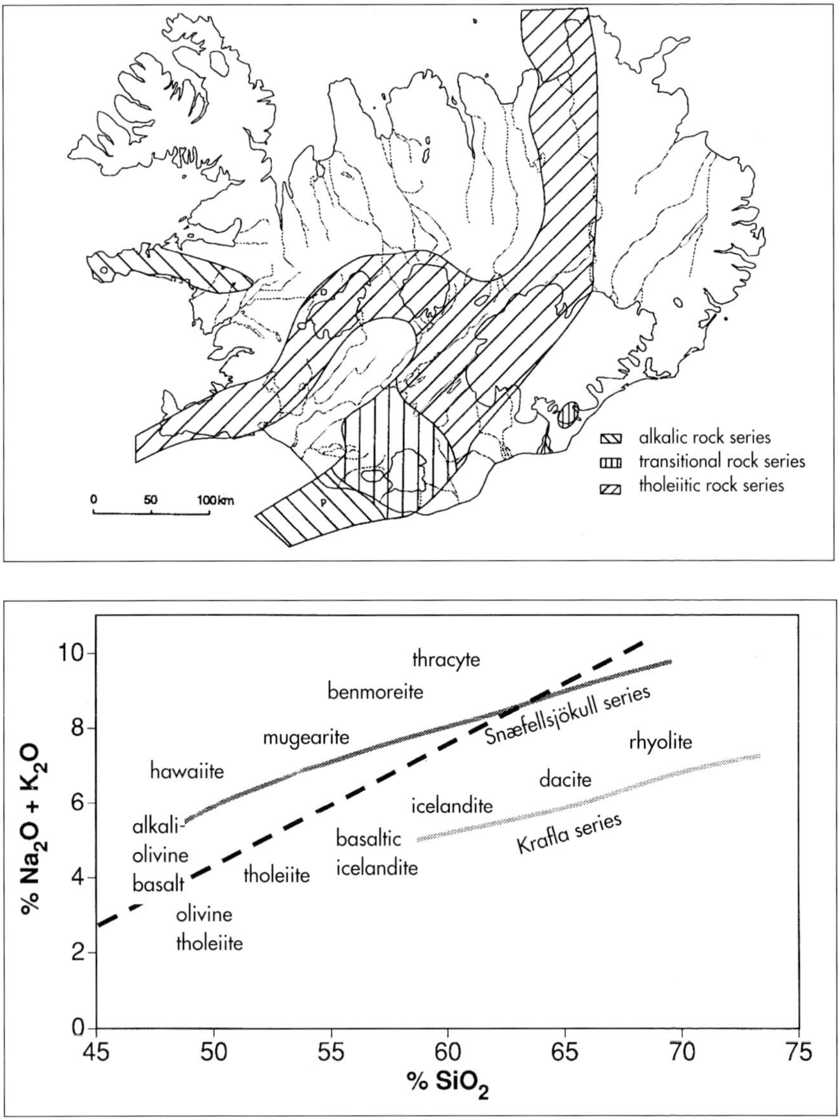

90. The map shows the regional variation of the chemical composition of magmatic rocks in Iceland. The tholeiitic series is confined to the rift zone. The alkalic series is found in Snæfellsnes and in the Vestmannaeyjar area but the transitional series in South Iceland (a propagating rift-area). The diagram contains the stippled "Hawaiian boundary" between high-alkaline, nepheline-normative rocks and the low-alkaline, quartz-normative rocks. The rift-zone tholeiites evolve from an olivine-tholeiite primary magma towards tholeiite, basaltic icelandite, icelandite, dacite and finally rhyolite, shown by the series from the Krafla volcano. The alkali basalts evolve towards hawaiite, mugearite, benmoreite, trachyte and finally rhyolite, shown by the series from the Snæfellsjökull volcano.

events and they characterize rifting episodes. But tectonic events are often followed by or associated with volcanic events, i.e. different kinds of eruptions. The term volcano-tectonic event or episode is used for an event or a whole episode of such combined activity.

An example of all this is the 2,800-3,000-year-long Hverfjall Period in the Krafla Volcanic System, consisting of 6 volcano-tectonic episodes and some tectonic episodes, each separated by up to hundreds of years. The second last volcano-tectonic episode occurred in 1724-1729 (the Mývatn Fires). The latest volcano-tectonic episode is the Krafla Fires in 1975-1984. It included inter alia 9 volcano-tectonic events (fissure eruptions), following a series of purely tectonic events. Some 3,000-4,000 years separate the Hverfjall Period from the Lúdent Period which included similar episodes in the Krafla Volcanic System.

■ The basalt variety

The magmatic rocks in Iceland, to a very large extent, belong to a single family of volcanic surface rocks called basalt. Basalt is the common product of oceanic volcanism. In Iceland, it is derived from partial melting (at approx. 1240°C) of the upper mantle rock which is most likely peridotite. The influence of the local hot spot makes, however, some of the Icelandic basalt different from common oceanic basalt.

Basalt comprises a range of basic rocks if defined according to the content of silica dioxide. Other families or groups of magmatic rocks defined on a similar basis are intermediate rocks (such as andesite or icelandite) and acid rocks (such as dacite or rhyolite). Both these latter groups exist in Iceland and account for approximately 10% of the bedrock, mainly as lava flows, compared to nearly 90% basalt. The acid rocks are usually light-coloured. Acid and intermediate rocks may develop from primary, basaltic magma by various processes.

Another method of grouping defines three rock series according to ratios of certain chemical substances. Each series still includes basic, intermediate and acid rocks, defined as above. The series are termed the tholeiitic series, the transitional series and the alkalic series (Fig. 90). Most volcanic rocks in Iceland stem from the tholeiitic series: tholeiite basalt and olivine tholeiite. They occur in fine-grained, dark-coloured lavas, dykes and sills. Local pressure and temperature conditions and the composition of the rock undergoing partial melting determine to which series the final melt will belong.

The volcanic rocks on the Earth's surface have relatives; coarse-grained magmatic rocks which solidify below the Earth's surface. The most common of such intrusive or plutonic rocks in Iceland are gabbro (related to basalt) and granophyre (related to rhyolite). These rocks are a minor part of the bedrock and occur in large intrusive bodies, most of which are former magma chambers.

The youngest Icelandic rocks occur within the active volcanic zone. The newest lava from Hekla is nearly 2 years old at the time of writing. Growing successively older and extending outwards from this zone, the oldest dated rocks in Iceland are found in the far northwest and east (Fig. 91). They are from 13 to nearly 15 million years old, making Iceland a mere infant among 3,500 million-year-old continental regions.

■ The volcanoes and their sources

Geophysical measurements reveal an abnormally hot, up-doming and ductile layer in the upper mantle beneath Iceland; earthquake waves slow down, the deep-earth resistivity is low and pronounced gravity anomalies indicate upwelling and hot mantle material (Fig. 92). The data is interpreted in favour of a layered mantle containing 5-20% partial melt. The melt fraction is derived from the mantle material which wells up everywhere beneath the Mid-Atlantic Ridge and from the partial melt within the local mantle plume. The layer is 8-10 km below the surface in the volcanic zone but at a 10-35 km-depth below the adjacent Quaternary and Tertiary areas (Fig. 93).

When hot mantle material rises and the rock pressure (static pressure) decreases, melting occurs. It is believed that small amounts of melt in minute "pockets" separate continuously from the creeping and partially molten "mush" in the mantle plume. A similar process also produces melt in the par-

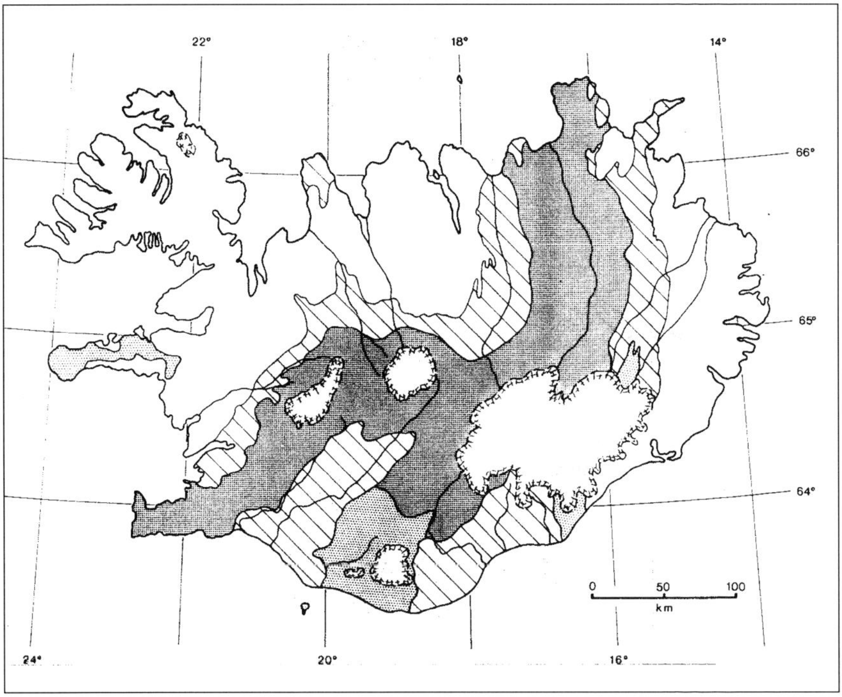

91. A simplified geological map of Iceland. The white areas mark the Tertiary rocks (lava flows, interbeds and intrusions), about 3.2-14 million years old. Areas with inclined lines are the Lower Pleistocene rocks (incl. lava flows and palagonite tuff), 0.72-3.1 million years old. The dotted areas represent the Upper Pleistocene rocks and the Holocene rocks, younger than 0.72 million years old (incl. lava flows and palagonite tuff). Dark areas denote the tholeiite series and light-dotted areas the locations of rocks from the alkalic and transitional series. (Various sources)

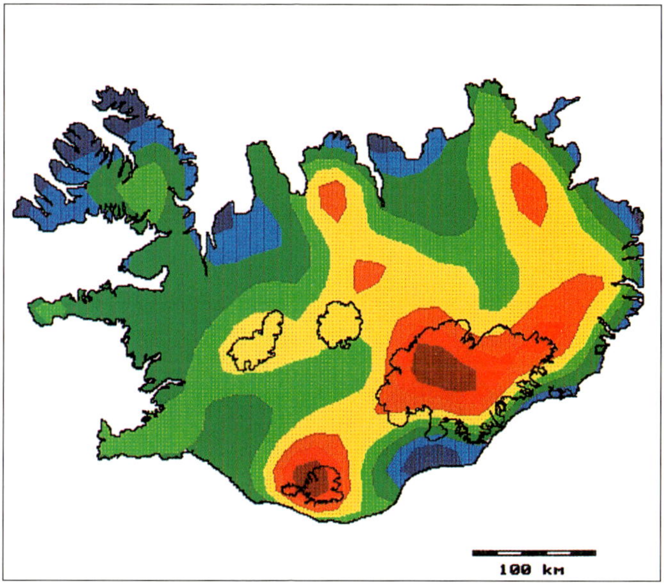

92. A map of gravity anomalies in Iceland. The high negative values centred at the large ice caps and in the north are interpreted as lightweight material rising in the mantle and the crust.

tially molten layer which is normally found everywhere beneath the Mid-Atlantic Ridge.

The melt pockets join into bigger and bigger channels on their way upwards which, in turn, end up as feeders for large "pools" of magma at the tops of elongated "caverns" (reservoirs) at the

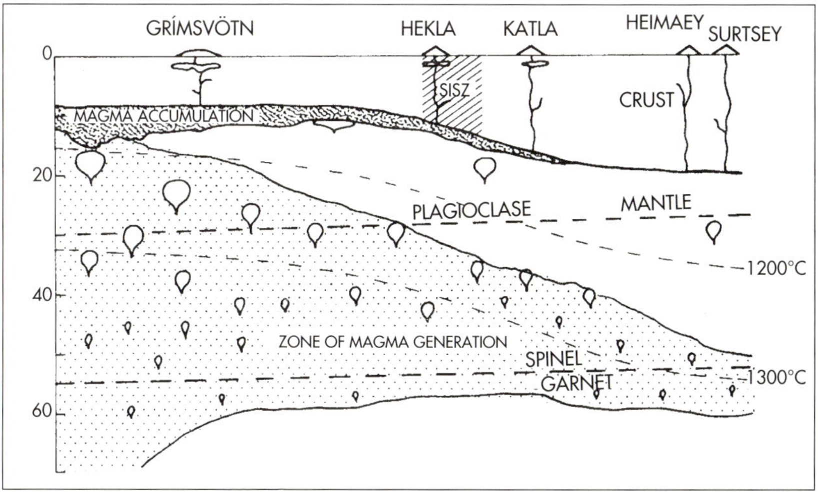

93. A schematic cross-section of the crust and mantle beneath the South Iceland Volcanic Zone; along a line from Surtsey to Grímsvötn. This is also a representative model of magma generation and accumulation in reservoirs and magma chambers.

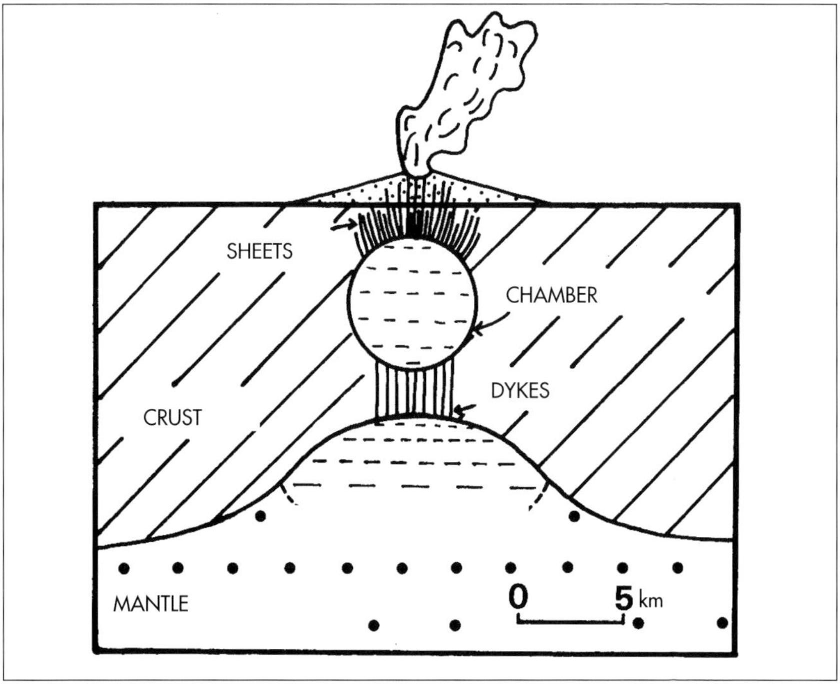

94. A schematic cross-section showing a magma reservoir and a magma chamber. The reservoir underlies more or less the whole length of a fissure swarm included in an elongated volcanic system. The reservoir top section is completely melted. A much smaller magma chamber is located in the crust above the central parts of the reservoir. Dykes supply magma from the reservoir to the magma chamber, but the magma can also surface in an eruption in the fissure swarm. The magma in the chamber is injected into the crust or emerges at a volcanic centre.

crust-mantle boundary. At lower levels, the reservoirs contain partially molten rock (probably 5-20% melt), which grades into the more or less totally molten top-layers. There are numerous such magma reservoirs in the upper section of the partially molten layer beneath Iceland, underlying the volcanic zone. Their volume may range from a few hundred to several thousand cubic kilometres. Magma may ascend from the reservoirs, either directly to the surface fissure swarms above them, or into crustal magma chambers (at a 2-6 km-depth). Magma chambers develop from dense dyke swarms or plutonic bodies. The volumes of such chambers are in the order of 10-100 km^3 (Fig. 94).

As already mentioned, some of the magma escapes from magma reservoirs. In this case, the extruded magma rises through the crust as dykes due to high excess magma pressure. The melt may open up entirely new fissures but it commonly flows along weakness planes in the crust created by the stresses from plate spreading. The magma in magma chambers also builds up excess pressure due to a more or less continuous in-flow from beneath. The magma within a particular magma chamber is then periodically injected into the crust to form dykes, some of which reach the surface, leading to an eruption. In this case, dykes may create their own fissures, flow along old fissures or penetrate contact planes between old dykes and the host rock, resulting in the formation of multiple dykes.

The magma injections and the volcanic eruptions are often triggered by rifting events associated with plate movements. A high magma pressure may, however, induce an eruption, independent of divergent plate movements.

Different and complicated processes take place in the magma chambers. Remelting (host rock assimilation), magma mixing, fractional crystallization (some magma solidifies and the rest is chemically changed) and liquid fractionation (light and heavy material is separated) produce a range of evolved magmas. Commonly, acid and intermediate magmas form in the magma chambers. Thus, a single magma chamber may supply both basalt and acid rocks such as dacite to the same volcano. Similar processes occur within the magma reservoirs but reservoirs generally tend to produce evolved types of basalt only.

■ Types of volcanoes and volcanic eruptions

Volcanic eruptions are either mixed (both lava and tephra) or effusive (mostly lava) or phreatic/explosive (tephra only). In all cases, the magma contains volcanic gases (water vapour is dominant). The tendency to explosive activity increases as magma becomes more acid. Water and glacial ice can also enhance explosive volcanism.

There are three main categories of volcanoes in Iceland:

1. Central volcanoes located above the magma chambers and built up during repeated closely spaced eruptions. They sometimes develop into high mountains with summit craters (stratovolcanoes, Fig. 49 and 80). Alternatively, a central volcano may become a mountain massif with a circular subsiding area (a caldera, Fig. 54) above its magma chamber, and many fissures. The magmas range from basalts to acid rocks.

2. Lava shields, which erupt only once and are thought to be fed directly from magma reservoirs in the upper mantle. These structures are relatively flat lava domes (Fig. 28) with a central crater. The lava flows are made of basalts; including picrites and olivine-tholeiites.

3. Volcanic fissures, which are short or long rows of craters ranging from spatter cones and scoria craters (Fig. 26 and 71) to tephra rings and maars (explosion vents, Fig. 83). A nearby magma chamber or a deeper-lying reservoir supplies the magma, most of which is of the basaltic type.

An attempt to classify basaltic volcanoes and volcanic vents is found on page 116. The table, along with the aforementioned central volcanoes, illustrates that examples of almost every known type of volcano in the world are found in Iceland.

■ A zone never at ease

The active volcanic zone in Iceland includes the longest exposed rifting

GEOMORPHIC CLASSIFICATION OF ICELANDIC BASALT VOLCANOES

NATURE OF VOLCANIC ACTIVITY	ENVIRONMENT DURING FORMATION	FORM OF FEEDER CONDUIT: SHORT FISSURE OR TUBULAR CONDUIT	FORM OF FEEDER CONDUIT: LONG FISSURE
EFFUSIVE ACTIVITY – Landforms resulting form flowing material	subaerial	LAVA RING Type: Eldborg (Hnappadalssýsla)	–
		LAVA SHIELD Type: Skjaldbreidur	LAVA SHIELD ROW Type: Thjófahraun
MIXED ACTIVITY Landforms resulting from flowing material and hyaloclastites	Subglacial/ subaerial	TABLE MOUNTAIN (STAPI) Type: Herdubreid	SUBGLACIAL RIDGE Type: Kálfstindar
	Submarine/ Subaerial	TABLE MOUNTAIN (STAPI) Type: Surtsey	–
	Submarine	SEAMOUNT Type: Jólnir	SUBMARINE RIDGE Type: Eldeyjarbodi
	Subglacial	* Type: Keilir	* Type: Fögrufjöll
Landforms resulting from flowing and airborne material	Subaerial	SPATTER CONE Type: Búrfell (Hafnarfjördur)	SPATTER CONE ROW Types: Threngslaborgir
		SCORIA CONE Type: Búdaklettur	SCORIA COEN ROW Type: Vikraborgir
		–	MIXED CONE ROW Type: Lakagígar
EXPLOSIVE (OR PHREATO-MAGMATIC) ACTIVITY Landforms resulting from airborne material	Subaerial	TEPHRA RING Type: Hverfjall	TEPHRA RING ROW Type: Vatnaöldur
		MAAR Type: Graenavatn	MAAR ROW Type: Valagjá

*The two landforms marked * have no terms in English but are the subglacial counterparts to a single subaerial cone and a mixed cone row, respectively.*

ridge segments or diverging plate boundaries (400 km) in the world. This neovolcanic zone is composed of one, slightly bent, main rift zone. It runs from the southwest, where the submarine Reykjanes Ridge meets Iceland, to the northeast where it is terminated by a fracture zone at sea (Tjörnes Fracture Zone) in Öxarfjörður. This NW-SE-trending fracture zone separates the Iceland Rift Zone from still another rift zone segment, the Kolbeinsey Ridge, which runs northwards from Iceland (Fig. 42). In addition there are at least

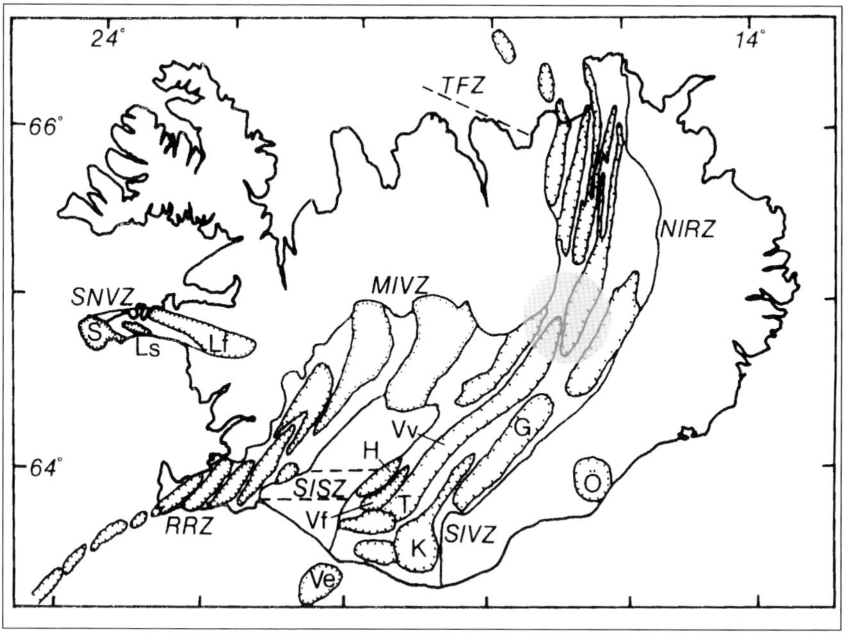

95. The neovolcanic zone of Iceland is a trace of the divergent plate boundaries of the Mid-Atlantic Ridge across Iceland. It comprises, however, not only a rift zone but also flank zones as well as fracture zones. RRZ: Reykjanes Rift Zone. SISZ: South Iceland Seismic Zone. SIVZ (or EVZ): South Iceland Volcanic Zone (or the Eastern Volcanic Zone). MIZV: Mid-Iceland Volcanic (or Rift) Zone. NIRZ: Northeast Iceland Rift Zone. SNVZ: Snæfellsnes Volcanic Zone. TFZ: Tjörnes Fracture Zone. Dotted contours denote volcanic systems. The centre of the hot spot is marked with a shaded dot.

two non-rifting flank zones (Fig. 95). The total area of the neovolcanic zone is 26,000 km^2. The individual zones are termed as:

1. The Icelandic Rift Zone (IRZ) is split up into two sections; the Reykjanes Rift Zone (RRZ) and the Northeast Iceland Rift Zone (NIRZ). Between them, in central Iceland, is a volcanic region comprising the Langjökull and Hofsjökull volcanic systems. Being made of tholeiitic rocks it is usually included in the IRZ (split up into the IRZ and the NIRZ), but some prefer to treat it as a separate volcanic zone, termed the Mid-Iceland Volcanic Zone (MIVZ).
2. The non-rifting Snæfellsnes Volcanic Zone (SNVZ)
3. The non-rifting South Iceland Volcanic Zone (SIVZ) which is of transient nature as the NIRZ seems to be propagating slowly southwards into the SIVZ. Many use the term Eastern Volcanic Zone (EVZ).

A third flank zone may exist. It includes the Öræfajökull volcano, the Esjufjöll volcano and Snæfell, all in an elongated area east of the SIVZ and NIRZ.

Tholeiitic rocks dominate the rift zone (ranging from basalt to very acid

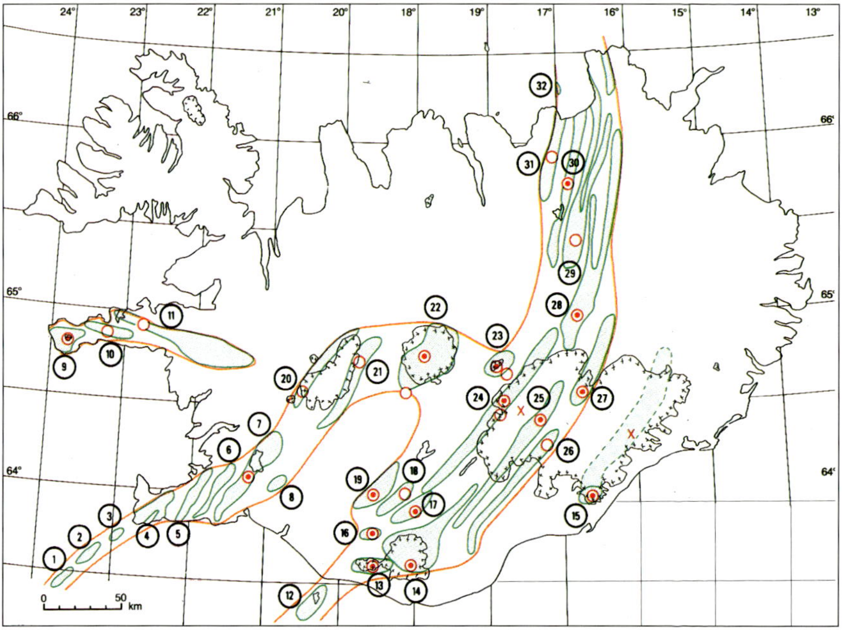

96. The Icelandic volcanic systems. Double dots represent prominent central volcanoes. The circles represent volcanic centres without prominent volcanic structures or structures hidden by ice. An X marks an uncertain centre. The names of the volcanic systems are listed below, from 1-32. In a few cases one number denotes two individual centres, the latter being an uncertain or debated one.

1. Eldeyjarboði
2. Geirfuglasker
3. Eldey
4. Reykjanes
5. Trölladyngja (or Krísuvík)
6. Brennisteinsfjöll
7. Hengill
8. Grímsnes
9. Snæfellsjökull
10. Lýsuskarð
11. Ljósufjöll
12. Vestmannaeyjar
13. Eyjafjallajökull
14. Katla
15. Öræfajökull
16. Tindfjallajökull
17. Torfajökull
18. Vatnafjöll
19. Hekla
20. Langjökull I
21. Langjökull II
22. Hofsjökull and Kerlingarfjöll (to the South)
23. Tungnafellsjökull and Vonarskarð (to the Southeast)
24. Bárðarbunga and Hamarinn (to the Southwest)
25. Grímsvötn and Loki (to the Northwest)
26. Þórðarhyrna
27. Kverkfjöll and Esjufjöll (to the Southeast)
28. Dyngjufjöll
29. Fremri-Námur
30. Krafla and Heiðarsporður (to the East)
31. Þeistareykir
32. Mánáreyjar

rocks), but the transitional and alkalic rocks are found in the flank zones (also ranging from basalt to acid rocks, Fig. 90). This regional distribution has been explained as follows:

* *Partial* melting beneath the rift zone occurs at high temperature but relatively low pressure. The low-alkali melt is tholeiitic basalt which may evolve in reservoirs to intermediate and acid magmas.

* *Partial* melting occurs at greater depth beneath the flank zones. Higher pressure and less partial melting favour the production of magmas from the alkalic series (Snæfellsnes and Vestmannaeyjar).

* *Magmas* from the transitional series may be generated by remelting of the tholeiitic crustal rocks containing water and by mixing this melt with ascending tholeiitic magma. Alternatively, the transitional series is a product of primary alkali basalt or a primary olivine tholeiite melting and assimilating the base of the crust (the region between Hekla and Katla).

■ 30 volcanic systems

The active and dormant volcanoes, volcanic fissures, tectonic fissures and faults are not scattered at random in the volcanic zone. They tend to form elongated areas, in a subparallel arrangement (en echelon). Each area comprises many tectonic fissures and normal faults (also en echelon), constituting a fissure swarm, as well as many volcanic structures. The fissure swarm and small or large volcanic structures are assumed to be a surface manifestation of the underlying magma reservoir. Most of these areas include a central volcano (plus an associated magma chamber) and many display a centrally located graben. The areas are termed volcanic systems and number about 30 within the neovolcanic zone (Fig. 96). At least 10 have developed distinct calderas within the rift zone proper and four volcanic systems in the flank zones are crowned by large stratovolcanoes. Some lava shields are found within most of the systems in the rift zone but others are located in their vicinity. Some volcanic systems are partly covered by ice caps and glaciers. Most fissure swarms are 40-100 km long and 10-30 km wide.

A mature volcanic system (Fig. 97) has many distinct features. Its highest part, the volcanic centre or high-production focus, is located directly above a magma chamber (or a reservoir). High-temperature geothermal activity and acid rock outcrops are common at the centre. The centre is usually cut by a tectonic fissure swarm which can extend farther from the centre than any of its eruptive fissures. Repeated eruptions deposit lava and tephra at the centre as magma ascends through old vents and fresh fissures from the magma chamber (or reservoir). The fissure in-fills often form cone sheets or ring-dykes in the crust above it, in association with a caldera subsidence.

Outside the central volcano, magma may ascend through fissures to the surface or be injected into the crust without ever surfacing, but forming dykes in both cases. Some of this magma flows laterally to some extent, in fissures from the central magma chamber. Magma may, however, also rise vertically from the underlying reservoir into the fissure swarm, giving rise to eruptions far away from the centre, but within the fissure swarm (Fig. 98).

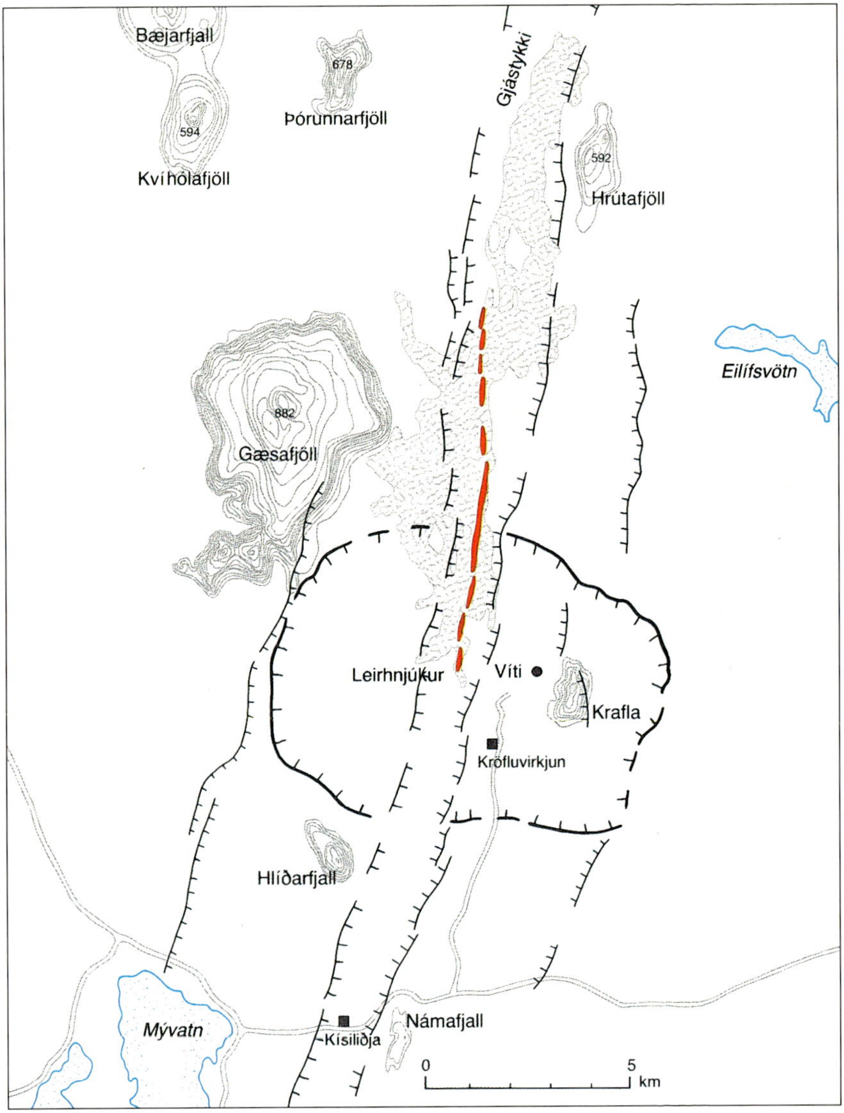

97. A mature volcanic system (Krafla Volcanic System). Most volcanic systems include a fissure swarm with open fissures and normal faults (not all shown); commonly prominent as a graben (here, the Gjástykki). Volcanic fissures are aligned with different craters, represented here with the crater row and lava flow from 1984. The volcanic centre is a cluster of hills and mountains made of tuff, lava and acid rocks, set with a caldera, 5-7 km across. Leirhnúkur and Krafla are small hills and Víti a maar from 1724. A magma chamber is located at a depth of 3-7 km beneath the caldera and a larger reservoir still deeper down. Magma may ascend from the chamber to the surface within or close to the caldera but from the reservoir farther out in the fissure swarm.

98. A typical fissure eruption away from the centre of a volcanic system. Krafla 1981.
(Photo: Ómar Þ. Ragnarsson)

The volcanic activity is controlled by pressure changes in each chamber or reservoir. Such changes are partly caused by plate movements and partly by long-time, steady in-flow of magma into the magma store or by sudden changes of the in-flow. Increased magmatic pressure usually makes parts of a volcanic system inflate, which is followed by a deflation if magma leaves the source. Earth tremors accompany these movements, especially the more sudden deflation. All those features enable scientists to monitor volcanoes, and sometimes to predict eruptions.

Selected References

The following list of references is limited to a few sources for each chapter of the book. The books and scientific papers contain further references. The two main journals in Iceland which publish writings on volcanic history are Jökull and Náttúrufræðingurinn, both with an English summary. The names of Icelandic authors are spelled in English (æ as ae, ö as ö, þ as th and ð as d and a, o, i, u instead of á, ó, í, ú).

KRAFLA AND VICINITY (Chapter 1)

Björnsson A., 1985: "Dynamics of crustal rifting in NE Iceland". *J. Geophys.*, 47., pp. 184-190.

Einarsson P., 1978: "S-wave shadows in the Krafla caldera in NE-Iceland, evidence for a magma chamber in the crust". *Bull. volcanol.* 41., pp. 1-9.

Einarsson P., 1991: "Umbrotin við Kröflu 1975-89", in: *Náttúra Mývatns*, eds. Gardarsson, A. and Einarsson, A., Hið ísl. náttúrufræðifélag, pp. 96-140, Reykjavík.

Lacasse C., Sigurdsson H., Johannesson H., Paterne M. and Carey S.: "The source of Ash Zone 1 in the North Atlantic". *Bull Volc.* (in print.) 1995.

Saemundsson K., 1991: "Jarðfræði Kröflukerfisins", in: *Náttúra Mývatns*, eds. Garðarsson A., and Einarsson, A., Hið ísl. náttúrufræðifélag, pp. 24-96, Reykjavík.

Tryggvason E., 1984: "Widening of the Krafla fissure swarm during the 1975-1981 volcano-tectonic episode". *Bull. Volcanol.*, 47., pp. 97-118.

GRÍMSVÖTN (Chapter 2)

Björnsson H., 1988: "Hydrology of ice caps in volcanic regions". *Soc. Sci. Isl.*, 45., 139 pp. Reykjavík.

Grönvold K. and Johannesson H., 1984: "Eruption in Grímsvötn 1983; course of events and chemical studies of the tephra". *Jökull*, 34., pp 1-11.

Gudmundsson M. T., 1989: "The Grímsvötn caldera, Vatnajökull: subglacial topography and structure of caldera infill". *Jökull*, 39., p. 1-21.

Gudmundsson M.T. and Björnsson H., 1991: "Eruptions in Grímsvötn, Vatnajökull, Iceland, 1934-1991". *Jökull*, 41., pp. 21-46.

Gudmundsson M.T., Björnsson H. and Palsson F., 1995: "Changes in jökulhlaup sizes in Grímsvötn, Vatnajökull, Iceland, 1934-91, deduced from in-situ measurements of subglacial lake volume". *J. of Glaciol.*, 41, no. 138, pp. 263-272.

Thorarinsson S., 1974: *Vötnin stríð. Saga Skeiðarárhlaupa og Grímsvatnagosa.* 254 pp. Reykjavík.

VESTMANNAEYJAR (Chapter 3)

Einarsson Th., 1973: *The eruption of Heimaey.* Mál og menning. Reykjavík.

Jakobsson S. P., 1979: "Petrology of recent basalts of the Eastern Volcanic Zone, Iceland". *Act. Nat. Isl.*, Vol. II, 103 pp. Reykjavík.

Thorarinsson S., 1966: *Surtsey: the new island in the North Atlantic.* Almenna bókafélagið. 47 pp. Reykjavík.

Thorarinsson S., Steinthorsson S., Einarsson T., Kristmannsdóttir H., Oskarsson N., 1973: "The eruption of Heimaey, Iceland". *Nature*, 241., pp. 372-375.

Norrman, J. O. and Erlingsson V.: "The Submarine morphology of Surtsey volcanic group". *Surtsey Res. Progr. Report* 10, pp. 45–56. 1992.

HENGILL, ÞINGVELLIR AND SKJALDBREIÐUR (Chapter 4)

Gudmundsson A., 1987: "Tectonics of the Thingvellir fissure swarm, SW Iceland". *J. Struct. Geol.*, vol. 9, no. 1, pp. 61-69.

Saemundsson K., 1967: "Vulkanismus und Tektonik des Hengill-Gebietes in Südwest-Island". *Act. Nat. Isl.*, Vol.II, 115 pp. Reykjavík.

Saemundsson K., 1992: "Geology of the Thingvallavatn area". *OIKOS 64.*, Copenhagen, pp. 40-68.

REYKJANES PENINSULA (Chapter 5)

Gudmundsson A., 1986: "Mechanical aspects of postglacial volcanism and tectonics of the Reykjanes Peninsula, SW Iceland". *J. geophys. Res.*, 91, pp. 12,711-12,721.

Gudmundsson A., 1987: "Geometry, formation and development of tectonic fractures on the Reykjanes Peninsula, SW-Iceland". *Tectonophysics,* 139., pp. 295-308.

Jakobsson S. P., Jonson J.,

Shido F., 1978: "Petrology of the western Reykjanes Peninsula, Iceland". *J. Petrol.*, 19., pp. 669-705.

Johannesson H. and Einarsson S., 1988: "Krísuvíkureldar I: Aldur Ögmundarhrauns og miðaldalagsins". *Jökull*, 38., pp. 71-88.

Einarsson S., Johannesson H. and Sveinbjörnsdottir A. E., 1991: "Krísuvíkureldar II. Kapelluhraun og gátan um aldur Hellnahrauns". *Jökull*, 41., pp. 61-81.

Sigurgeirsson, M. A., 1995: "Yngra-Stampagosið á Reykjanesi". *Náttúrufræðingurinn* 64, pp. 211–230.

Saemundsson, K., 1992: "Hellisheiðahraun". Orkustofnun, Jarðhitadeild KS-92/01. 14p.

TABLE MOUNTAINS, TUFF RIDGES, LAVA SHIELDS (Chapter 6)

Saemundsson K., 1979: "Outline of the geology of Iceland". *Jökull*, 29., pp. 7-28.

Walker G. P. L., 1965: "Some aspects of Quaternary volcanism". *Trans. Leicester Lit. Phil. Soc.*, 59., pp. 25-40.

HOFSJÖKULL AND VICINITY (Chapter 7)

Björnsson H., 1988: "Hydrology of ice caps in volcanic regions". *Soc. Sci. Isl.*, 45., 139 pp. Reykjavík.

GRÍMSNES (Chapter 8)

Jakobsson S. P., 1966: "The Grimsnes lavas, SW-Iceland". *Act. Nat. Isl.*, Vol. II, 30 pp. Reykjavík.

ÞEISTAREYKIR AND VICINITY (Chapter 9)

Armannsson H., Gislason G. and Torfason H., 1986: "Surface exploration of the Theistareykir high-temperature geothermal area, Iceland, with special reference to the application of geochemical methods". *Appl. Geochem.*, Vol. 1, pp. 47-64.

KATLA AND ELDGJÁ (Chapter 10)

Björnsson H. and Palsson F., 1994: Mýrdalsjökull: "Yfirborð, botn og rennslisleiðir jökulhlaupa við gos undir jöklinum". Abstracts from a symposium "Kötlustefna". Reykjavík, pp. 3.

Einarsson E., Larsen G., Thorarinsson S., 1980: "The Sólheimar tephra layer and the Katla eruption of 1357". *Act. Nat. Isl.*, publication nr. 28., 24 pp. Reykjavík.

Jonsson J., 1978: "Eldstöðvar og hraun í Skaftafellsþingi". *Náttúrufræðingurinn*, 48., pp. 196-232.

Larsen G., 1979: "Um aldur Eldgjárhrauna". *Náttúrufræðingurinn*, 49., pp. 1-25.

Larsen G., 1993: "Nokkur orð um Kötlugos og Kötlugjósku". Abstracts from a symposium on Katla. The Science Institute of the University of Iceland, Reykjavík, pp. 6-8.

Thorarinsson S., 1975: "Katla og annáll Kötlugosa". *Árbók Ferðafélags Íslands*. Reykjavík.

EYJAFJALLAJÖKULL (Chapter 11)

Jakobsson S. P., 1979: "Petrology of recent basalts of the Eastern Volcanic Zone, Iceland". *Act. Nat. Isl.*, Vol. II, 103 pp. Reykjavík.

Johannesson H., 1985: "Um endasleppu hraunin undir Eyjafjöllum og jökla síðasta jökulskeiðs". *Jökull*, 35., pp. 83-95.

ASKJA AND VICINITY (Chapter 12)

Bäckstrom K. and Gudmundsson A., 1989: "The grabens of Sveinar and Sveinagja, NE Iceland". *Nordic Volc. Inst.* publ. nr. 8901., 38 pp. Reykjavík.

Brandsdottir B., 1992: "Historical accounts of earthquakes associated with eruptive activity in the Askja Volcanic System". *Jökull*, 42., pp. 1-12.

Sigurdsson H. and Sparks R. S. J., 1978: "Rifting episode in North Iceland in 1874-1875 and the eruptions of Askja and Sveinagjá". *Bull. Volcanol*, 41, pp. 149-167.

Sigvaldason G. E., 1981: "Um jarðfræði Ódáðahrauns". *Árbók Ferðafélags Íslands*, pp. 156-177, Reykjavík.

Sigvaldason G.E., Annertz K. and Nilsson M., 1992: "Effect of glacier loading/deloading on volcanism: postglacial volcanic production rate of the Dyngjufjöll area, central Iceland". *Bull. Volcanol.*, 54., pp. 385-392.

Thorarinsson S. and Sigvaldason G., 1962: "The eruption in Askja, 1961. A preliminary report". *Am. J. Sci.*, 260, pp. 641-651.

HEKLA AND VICINITY (Chapter 13)

Jakobsson S. P., 1979: "Petrology of recent basalts of the Eastern Volcanic Zone, Iceland". *Act. Nat. Isl.*, Vol.II, 103 pp. Reykjavík.

Kjartansson E. and Grönvold K., 1983: "Location of a magma reservoir beneath Hekla volcano, Iceland". *Nature*, 301., pp. 139-141.

Larsen G. and Thorarinsson S.,

1977: "H4 and other acid Hekla tephra layers". *Jökull*, 27., pp. 2-27.

Grönvold K., Larsen G., Einarsson P., Thorarinsson S., Saemundsson K., 1983: "The Hekla eruption 1980-1981". *Bull. Volcanol.*, vol. 46., pp. 349-363.

Gudmundsson A., Oskarsson N., Groenvold K., Saemundsson K., Sigurdsson O., Stefansson R., Gislason S.R., Einarsson P., Brandsdottir B., Larsen G., Johannesson H. and Thordarson Th., 1992: "The 1991 eruption of Hekla, Iceland". *Bull. Volcanol.*, 54., pp. 238-246.

Thorarinsson S., 1967: "The eruptions of Hekla in historical times", in: *The Eruption of Hekla 1947-48*, 1, pp. 1-170. Soc. Sci. Isl. Reykjavík.

TORFAJÖKULL AND VICINITY (Chapter 14)
Arnorsson S., Ivarsson G., Cuff K. E., and Saemundsson K., 1987: "Geothermal activity in the Torfajökull field, S-Iceland; summary of geothermal studies". *Jökull*, 37., pp. 1-10.

Ivarsson G., 1993: "Torfajökull. Jarðfræði og bergefnafræði. Abstracts of the spring symposium of the Union of Icelandic Geoscientists in April 1993. Reykjavík, pp. 19-21.

Jakobsson S. P., 1979: "Petrology of recent basalts of the Eastern Volcanic Zone, Iceland". *Act. Nat. Isl.*, Vol. II, 103 pp. Reykjavík.

Saemundsson K., 1972: "Jarðfræðiglefsur um Torfajökulssvæðið". *Náttúrufræðingurinn*, 42., pp. 81-99.

Saemundsson K., 1988: "Jarðfræðiþáttur um Torfajökulssvæðið". *Árbók Ferðafélags Íslands*, Reykjavík, pp. 164-181.

KVERKFJÖLL AND VICINITY (Chapter 15)
Karhunen R., 1988: "Eruption mechanism and rheomorphism during the basaltic fissure eruption in Biskupsfell, Kverkfjöll, North-Central Iceland". *Nordic Volc. Inst.* publ. nr. 8802, 91 pp. Reykjavík.

Thorarinsson S., Saemundsson K. and Williams R. S., 1973: "ERTS-1 image of Vatnajökull. Analysis of glaciological structures and volcanic features". *Jökull*, 23., pp. 7-17.

ÖRÆFAJÖKULL (Chapter 16)
Prestvik T., 1982: "Petrography, chemical characteristics and nomenclature of Öraefajökull rocks". *Jökull*, 32., pp. 69-76.

Thorarinsson S., 1958: "The Öræfajökull eruption of 1362". *Act. Nat. Isl.*, Vol. II, 99 pp. Reykjavík.

LAKAGÍGAR (Chapter 17)
Sigmarsson O. and Condomines M., 1991: "Extreme magma homogenity in the 1783-1784 Lakagigar Eruption: origin of a large volume of evolved basalt in Iceland". *Geophys. Res. Lett.*, vol. 18, no. 12, pp. 2,229-2,232.

Sigurdsson H. and Sparks R. S. J., 1978: "Lateral magma flow within rifted Icelandic crust". *Nature*, 274., pp. 126-130.

Skaftáreldar 1783-1784. Eds. G. A. Gunnlaugsson, Thorarinsdottir, H. et al. Mál og menning. 380 pp. Reykjavík.

Thorarinsson S., 1969: "The Lakagígar Eruption of 1783". *Bull. Volcanol.*, Vol. 33., pp. 910-929.

Thordarson Th., 1990: "Skaftáreldar 1783-1784". Thesis. University of Iceland. Reykjavík. 187 pp.

BÁRÐARBUNGA, VEIÐIVÖTN AND VICINITY (Chapter 18)
Björnsson, H, 1988: "Hydrology of ice caps in volcanic regions". *Soc. Sci. Isl.*, 45., 139 pp. Reykjavík.

Hjartarson A., 1988: "Þjórsárhraunið mikla – stærsta nútímahraun jarðar". *Náttúrufræðingurinn*, 58., pp. 1-17.

Larsen G., 1984: "Recent volcanic history of the Veiðivötn fissure swarm, South Iceland. An approach to volcanic risk assessment". *J. of Volcanol. and Geot. Res.*, 22., pp. 33-58.

SNÆFELLSJÖKULL AND VICINITY (Chapter 19)
Johannesson H., 1980: "Jarðlagaskipan og þróun rekbelta á Vesturlandi". *Náttúrufræðingurinn*, 50., pp. 13-31.

Johannesson H., 1982: "Yfirlit um jarðfræði Snæfellsness". *Árbók Ferðafélags Íslands*. Reykjavík.

Johannesson H., Flores R. M., Jonsson J., 1981: "A short account of the Holocene tephrochronology of the Snaefellsjokull central volcano, W-Iceland". *Jökull*, 31., pp. 23-30.

VOLCANIC ACTIVITY IN ICELAND (chapter 20)
Beblo M., Björnsson A., Arnason K., Stein B. and Wolfgram P., 1983: "Electrical conductivity beneath Iceland – Constraints imposed by magnetotelluric results on temperature, partial melt, crust and mantle

structure". *Journ. of Geophys.*, 53., pp. 16-23.

Bjarnason I., Menke W., Flovenz O.G. and Caress D.: "Tomographic image of the spreading center in southern Iceland." *Journ. Geophys. Res.* 98., 1993, pp. 6, 607-6,622

Björnsson A., 1985: "Dynamics of crustal rifting in NE Iceland". *Journ. Geophys. Res.* 90., pp. 10,151-10,162.

Björnsson H., 1988: "Hydrology of ice caps in volcanic regions". *Soc. Scient. Isl.* no. 45., Reykjavík, 138 pp.

Björnsson H. and Einarsson P., 1990: "Volcanoes beneath Vatnajökull, Iceland: Evidence from radio echo-sounding, earthquakes and jökulhlaups". *Jökull*, 40., pp. 147-169.

Björnsson S., 1983: "Crust and upper mantle beneath Iceland". In: *Structure and Development of the Greenland-Scotland Ridge*, eds. Bott, Saxov, Talwani and Thiede. Plenum Press, New York, pp. 31-61.

Einarsson P. and Björnsson S., 1979: "Earthquakes in Iceland". *Jökull*, 29., pp. 37-43.

Einarsson P., 1991: "Earthquakes and present-day tectonism in Iceland". *Tectonophysics* 189., pp. 281-279.

Eysteinsson H. and Hermance J.F., 1985: "Magnetotelluric measurements across the Eastern Volcanic Zone in South Iceland". *Journ. of Geophys. Res.* 90., pp. 10,093-10,103.

Flovenz O.G. and Gunnarsson K., 1991: "Seismic crustal structure in Iceland and surrounding area". *Tectonophysics*, 189., pp. 1-17.

Flovenz O.G. and Saemundsson K., 1992: "Iceland". In: *Geothermal Atlas of Europe. Explanatory text.* Ed. by Hurtig E., Cermák V., Haenel R. and Zui A. Hermann Haack Verlag, pp. 48-51.

Gebrande H., Miller H. and Einarsson P., 1980: "Seismic structure of Iceland along RRISP-profile I". *Journ. Geophys.*, 47., pp. 239-249.

Grönvold K., 1988: "Krafla's lavas and lava composition within a fault swarm". Symp. on geol. and geochem. evidence for segmentation of continental and oceanic rifts. *Woods Hole*, abstract vol. 16.

Gudmundsson A., 1986: "Formation of crustal magma chambers in Iceland". *Geology*, 14., pp. 164-166.

Gudmundsson A., 1987. "Formation and mechanics of magma reservoirs in Iceland". *Geophys. J. R. Astr. Soc.* 91., pp. 27-41.

Jakobsson S.P.,1979: "Outline of the petrology of Iceland". *Jökull*, 29., pp. 57-73.

Oskarsson N., Steinthorsson S. and Sigvaldason G. E., 1985: "Iceland geochemical anomaly: origin, volcano-tectonics, chemical fractionation and isotope evolution of the crust". *Journ. Geophys. Res.* 90., (no.B 12), p. 10,011-10,025.

Palmason G., 1986: "Model of crustal formation in Iceland and application to submarine mid-ocean ridges". In: *The Geology of North America,* vol. M: the Western North Atlantic Region, ed. Vogt P.R. and Tucholke B.E., Geol. Soc. Am., pp. 87-97.

Saemundsson K., 1978: "Fissure swarms and central volcanoes of the neovolcanic zones of Iceland". *Geol. Journ.* Spec. Issue 10., pp. 415-432.

Saemundsson K., 1986: "Subaerial volcanism in the western North Atlantic", in *the Geology of North America*, vol. M: the Western North Atlantic Region, ed. Vogt P.R. and Tucholke B.E.. Geol. Soc. Am., pp. 69-86.

Sigmarsson O., Condomines M. and Fourcarde S., 1992: "Mantle and crustal contribution in the genesis of recent basalts from off-rift zones in Iceland: Constraints from Th, Sr and O isotopes". *Earth and Planet. Sci. Lett.*, 110., pp. 149-162.

Sigvaldason G., 1983: "Volcanic predictions in Iceland". In (eds): Tazieff H. and Sabroux J.C.: *Forecasting volcanic events. Developments in volcanology.* Elsevier.

Steinthorsson S., Oskarsson N., Arnorsson S., and Gunnlaugsson E.: "Metasomatism in Iceland 1987: Hydrothermal alteration and remelting of oceanic crust". In: *Chemical transport in metasomatic processes*, ed. H.C. Helgeson, D. Reidel Publ. Comp. pp. 355-387.

Thorarinsson S. and Saemundsson K., 1979: "Volcanic activity in historical time". *Jökull*, 29., pp. 29-32.

Vogt P.R., 1983: "The Icelandic mantle plume: status of the hypothesis after a decade of new work". In: *Structure and development of the Greenland-Scotland Ridge*, ed. Bott, Saxov, Talwani and Thiede. Plenum Publ. Comp. pp. 191-213.

References for Graphic Illustrations

FIG. 10, P. 21
Part of a map from: H. Björnsson and P. Einarsson, 1990, see reference list; based on a map by K. Saemundsson and P. Einarsson, 1987.

FIG. 11, P. 22
From: M. T. Gudmundsson, 1989: "The Grímsvötn Caldera, Vatnajökull: Subglacial topography and structure of caldera infill". *Jökull*, 39., pp. 1-21.

FIG. 13, P. 24
From: M. T. Gudmundsson and H. Björnsson, 1991: "Eruptions in Grímsvötn, Vatnajökull, Iceland 1901-1990". *Jökull*, 41, pp. 21–46.

FIG. 14, P. 26
Modified from: H. Björnsson, 1977: "The cause of jökulhlaups in the Skaftá river, Vatnajökull". *Jökull*, 27., pp. 71–78.

FIG. 17, P. 30
Mainly based on: S. P. Jakobsson, 1968: "The geology and petrography of the Vestmann Islands. A preliminary report". *Surtsey Res. Prog. Rep.* 4, pp. 113-129.

FIG. 21, P. 35
Compiled from data from: K. Saemundsson, 1967, see reference list, J. Jonsson, 1984: "Um heiðar og hraun", *Árbók Ferðafélags Íslands*, Reykjavík, G. Foulger, 1984, see reference list, and the Geol. Map issued by the Icel. Geodetic Surv. sheets 3 and 6.

FIG. 25, P. 40
From A. Gudmundsson, 1986: "Mechanical aspects of postglacial volcanism and tectonics of the Reykjanes Peninsula, SW-Iceland". *Journ of Geophys. Res*, vol. 91, no. B12, pp. 12,711-12,721; various data sources.

FIG. 35, P. 52
From: H. Björnsson, 1990: "Hofsjökull: Landslag, ísforði og vatnasvæði". *Náttúrufræðingurinn* 60., 3., pp.113-126.

FIG. 41, P. 58
Modified from: Sturkell E., Brandsdottir B., Shimamura H. and Mochizuki M., 1992: "Seismic crustal structure along the Öxarfjörður trough at the eastern margin of the Tjörnes Fracture Zone". *Jökull*, 42., pp. 13-25.

FIG. 45, P. 62
From: A. T. Gudmundsson, 1986: *Íslandseldar*, Reykjavík; based on: H. Björnsson, 1977 in *Náttúrufræðingurinn* 47., vol. 3-4, K. Saemundsson, 1982 in *Eldur er í norðri*, Reykjavík (see fig. 63) and the Geol. Map issued by the Icel. Geodetic Surv., sheet 6.

FIG 52, P. 70
From: A. T. Gudmundsson, 1986: *Íslandseldar*, Reykjavík; based on: geol. map issued by the Icel. Geodetic Surv. and Mus. of Icel. Nat. Hist., sheet 6.

FIG. 55, P. 72
Part of a map from: G. E. Sigvaldason et al., 1991; see reference list.
FIG. 60, P. 80
From: A. Gudmundsson, N. Oskarsson et al., 1992, see reference list.

FIG. 66, P. 88
Based on: K. Saemundsson, 1982: "Öskjur á virkum eldfjallasvæðum á Íslandi". In (eds): Th. Einarsson et al.: *Eldur er í norðri*. pp. 221-241. Reykjavík.

FIG. 72, P. 96
Redrawn from: S. Thorarinsson, 1983: "Skaftáreldar", *Árbók Ferðafélags Íslands*, Reykjavík, and from: E. L. Sveinsdottir's and Th. Einarsson's map in: G. A. Gunnlaugsson (ed.): *Skaftáreldar 1783-1784*, Reykjavík, 1984.

FIG. 75, P. 99
A part of a map from: G. Larsen: "Veiðivötn og Veiðivatnagos á 15. öld", 1988. *Árbók Ferðafélags Íslands*, Reykjavík, p. 152.

FIG. 77, P. 101
Based on: G. Larsen, 1982: "Gjóskulagatímatal Jökuldals". In Th. Einarsson et al. (eds): *Eldur er í norðri*, Reykjavík, pp. 51-67, and Geol. Map. issued by the Icel. Geodetic Surv., sheet 6.

FIG. 78, P. 102
Based on: S. Thorarinsson and G. E. Sigvaldason, 1972: "Tröllagígar og Tröllahraun 1862-1864". Jökull 22., pp. 12-26

FIG. 79, P. 102
Modified from: A. Hjartarson, 1988: *Náttúrufræðingurinn*, 58. vol. 1, pp. 1-17.

FIG. 81,P. 104
Based on: Haukur Johannesson, 1982: "Yfirlit um jarðfæði Snæfellsness". *Árbók Ferðafélags Íslands*, Reykjavík.

FIG. 88,P. 111
From: P. Einarsson, 1986: "Seismicity along the eastern margin of the North American Plate". In: P.R. Vogt and B.E. Tucholke (eds): *The Geol. of*

North America. Vol. M. The Western North Atl. Region. The Geol. Soc. of America.

FIG. 89, P. 112
Modified from: S. Steinthorsson, 1986: "Ísland og heiti reiturinn". *Tímarit Háskóla Íslands*, 1.; based on G. E. Vink: "A hotspot model for Iceland and the Vöring Plateau", *Journ. Geophys. Res.*, vol. 87, no. B11, pp. 9,389-9,407.

FIG. 90, P. 114
Map based on S. P. Jakobsson, 1979, see reference list. Diagram from: S. Arnorsson, 1993: "Inngangur að bergfræði storkubergs". *Náttúrufræðingurinn*, 62., vol. 3-4., p. 197; based on data from P. Imsland, 1978: "The petrology of Iceland, some general remarks". *Nordic Volcanol. Inst. rep.* 7808 and N. Oskarsson et al., 1982: "A dynamic model of rift zone petrogenesis and the regional petrology of Iceland". *Journ. of Petrol.* 23., pp. 28-74.

FIG. 92, P. 117
From: S. Arnorsson, 1993: "Jarðhiti". *Náttúrufræðingurinn*, 63., vol. 1-2., pp. 39-56; map compiled by F. Thorarinsson.

FIG. 93, P. 117
From: P.S. Meyer et al., 1985: "Petrological and geochemical variations along Iceland's neovolcanic zones". *Journ. of Geophys. Res.*, vol. 90, No. B12, pp. 10,043-10,072,; based on data from G. Palmason 1971, 1973, G. Palmason et al. 1979. Angenheister et al. 1980, Hermance et al. 1975, Beblo and A. Björnsson, 1980, G. P. Hersir 1983; see reference list for more details.

FIG. 94, P. 118
Gudmundsson A. (A,C): "Dyke emplacements at divergent plate boundaries." In: (eds) Parker A.J., Rickwood P.C. and Tucker D.H.: *Mafic dykes and emplacement mechanism*. Balkema, Rotterdam, 1990, pp. 47–62.
Forslund T. and Gudmundsson A. (B): "Crustal spreading due to dykes and faults in Southwest Iceland," *Journ. Structural Geol.* vol 13, no. 4, 1991, 443-457.

FIG. 95, P. 121
Modified from: O. Sigmarsson, M. Condomines and S. Fourcade 1992; see reference list.

FIG 96, P. 122
Compiled from: A. T. Gudmundsson, 1986: Íslandseldar, Reykjavík, p. 62, and: H. Björnsson and P. Einarsson, 1990, see reference list.

FIG. 97, P. 124
Modified from: A. Björnsson et al., 1977, *Nature*, 266. and K. Saemundsson/O. Sigurdsson, 1984, *Skjálftabréf* nr. 59, the Science Institute of the University of Iceland.

TABLE P. 25
Based on: S. Thorarinsson, *1974: Vötnin stríð. Saga Skeiðarárhlaupa og Grímsvatnagosa.* 254 pp. Reykjavík.

TABLE P. 37
Compiled from data; see reference list on Hengill and vicinity (Chapter 4).

TABLE P. 42
Compiled from data; see reference list on Reykjanes peninsula (Chapter 5).

TABLE P. 54
From: S. P. Jakobsson, 1966: "The Grímsnes Lavas, SW-Iceland", *Act. Nat. Isl.* Vol. II, 30 pp. Reykjavík.

TABLE P. 66
From: G. Larsen 1993, see reference list, and based on S. Thorarinsson, 1975: "Katla og annáll Kötlugosa". *Árbók Ferðafélags Íslands*, Reykjavík.

TABLE P. 74
Compiled from data; see reference list on Askja and vicinity (Chapter 12).

TABLE P. 81
Based on: S. Thorarinsson, 1967: *The Hekla eruption 1947–1948:* "I. The eruptions of Hekla in historical times". Soc. sci. Islandica, Reykjavík, 170 pp.

TABLE P. 120
From: R. S. Williams, S. Thorarinsson and E. C. Morris 1983: "Geomorphic classification of Icelandic volcanoes". *Jökull*, 33., pp. 19-24.

Index

The Icelandic letter æ is listed as ae and Þ, Ö appear after X,Y,Z.